CAUGHT IN A WEB
BY A.J. SHAW

"We find out that life has a way of repeating itself without any help from us."

Preface

The End…OR… Another Beginning

Sounds of children splashing water in the bath; I sat in my chair, happy that for now we were safe.

Didi called out to me, "Dad! Catie is out of the bath, and Lilly is getting out, too."

"OK! I'll be right there!" I got up, walked into the bathroom, put Lilly's and Catie's pjs on, and told them to go to bed.

"Don't forget to tuck us in," they shouted.

"I won't," I answered as I went to help Didi out of the tub. You see, Didi was handicapped. She was born with spinal bifida. She never walked, but it did not stop her from doing anything she wanted. I picked her up out of the tub, dried her off, and put her diaper on. She had no control of her bowels or bladder.

I kissed her on the forehead, and she said to me, "Dad, I sure am glad to be home."

"Me too, Baby."

Didi crawled into their bedroom and I followed her. Her sisters were snuggled in bed, waiting on us. First, I gave Lilly a kiss, tucked her in and told her that I loved her. She echoed back that she loved me, too. Then I kissed Catie as Didi clambered into bed. After I kissed Catie, Didi kissed me. I turned out the light and said goodnight to all of them.

In chorus, they said, "It's good to be home, Dad. We love you."

"Love you, too. Now go to sleep."

We had many moments like that during those days. We were so happy to be together. The girls were in school, and they were excited to be with their friends. I hired a wonderful lady to help us at home. The girls and I went just about everywhere together.

One weekend, my parents watched the girls for me. They decided to go to their lake house. While there, Dad and Didi started down the steps of the house, and all at once, only the arms of the wheelchair were in Dad's hands. Didi went tumbling down the steps in the remaining part of the wheelchair. Dad had unknowingly forgotten to put the pins into the arms of the wheelchair. I know Dad felt a lot of guilt over that, but it could have happened to anybody. Didi was knocked out for awhile, so they rushed her to the hospital in Conway. After examining her, the doctor said Didi would be okay.

When they called to tell me about it, I told them to get her to Children's Hospital immediately. I met them there. The doctor found a blood clot, and they had to operate. Like a trooper, Didi took it all in stride. After she woke, she told me she was okay, and she wanted me to go on home and rest. The staff had always taken good care of her at the hospital. She was one of their pets. So I did as she asked and left.

On the way home, though, something was bugging me. I felt alone; I felt out of place and didn't know why.

That night happened to be election night, and our governor was running for president. I asked Mom and Dad to watch Catie and Lilly, and I drove back to Little Rock to see what was happening with the election. I had to park at the football stadium a few miles away and catch a bus to the old state capital downtown. People on the bus were excited and cheering for history was being made. I guess there were about sixty of us on the bus. When we arrived at the stop, I was one of the last off. As I walked toward the crowd, I lit a cigarette. About that time, the crowd roared! Bill Clinton had just won the election. I looked to the right and there were news trucks from all over the world. I looked to the left, and people were going crazy. It was history in the making! I took another puff off my cigarette and briefly closed my eyes. When my eyes opened, it was to see nothing but the lights of the old state capital, and all I heard was the wind blowing through the trees and the leaves being blown across the street. It was as if I was having an out-of-body experience. No news trucks, no people, only the lights of the old state capital, and the wind, and the leaves. As I got closer, Clinton and Gore and their wives came out of the old state house. It looked as if they were looking right at me with weird smiles on their faces, and then they waved goodbye. I turned and walked to the bus stop, waited a few minutes, and when the bus pulled up I got on and rode back to my car. The bus was only half full, unlike before. I got in my car, turned on the radio, and drove home. When I got home I was, to say the least, confused. I wondered if it even happened at all. So, I turned to the one thing that always helped me calm down…music. I picked Alan Parsons Project first album, put on the headphones, and as Orsen Wells started talking, I drifted into a dream within a dream.

CHAPTER 1
Times Were A'Changing

What does a person dream of when they're sleeping? Is it winning the lottery, hitting the jackpot at the casino? Maybe it's marrying the prom queen, or at least screwing her. Is it revenge; or happiness and contentment? I dreamed of only narrow-minded things. Looking back I realize that my dreams did not change between 1958 and 1967.
Also, looking back to 1958, something that stands out in my memory is gagging because the bathrooms on a ferry in Istanbul, Turkey were two footprints and a hole. I was too young to remember a lot of details of that trip with my parents, but that ferry's restroom is still a disgustingly vivid image in my head.
I remember wondering why my mother's voice was different than others in the south. Maybe pictures or stories I heard, or maybe just the sound of her voice told me that she was not from the south.
Scotland came up in conversations at my house many times. To me it was a land of my dreams, and a land where my sister was born. Around the age of eleven, my grandmother came from Scotland to

visit. Meeting her in itself planted something in me that is still a part of me today… a dream. It started opening the world to me.

A definite memory during those early years of my life was when my family took my grandmother to Canada while she was visiting America. On the way, I experienced places I would not have seen otherwise. I met my uncle and aunt in Canada, and I saw the biggest lake I'd ever seen. I saw the falls on the border of the U.S and Canada. What a trip! Then, I met my great-grandmother from Scotland who, I found out, raised my mother.

Later my family went on a dream trip, or so it seemed to me. We went on a jet plane to New York City. Wow! That was cool! Skyscapers reached the sky! Next, we rode a jet to Europe. We first landed in Ireland, then Scotland. That is where things all came together for me. I met my mother's family. I saw and heard my parents laugh and cry like I never before.

Like all trips, it was over too soon. What that adventure did for me was open a door to life like nothing else had before. Life was never the same. My eyes were opened, and could not be closed.

CHAPTER 2
Conway, Arkansas to Wynne, Arkansas

In 1968, things changed. Our family moved from what I thought was heaven on earth, Conway, Arkansas, to the armpit of the world, Wynne, Arkansas. As young kids in a small college town in the mid and late 1960s, we were too young for Woodstock, but old enough to remember exactly where we were when JFK was assassinated, and we were old enough to experience the gruesome imagery of the Vietnam War. We were old enough to identify the world's problems, but too young to do anything about it. In Conway, for young children from 8 to 10 years old, we had the luxury of free shows, kick the can, and neighborhood football games. During our adolescent years, Arkansas Razorback Football made its way into our lives and established a dynasty. We revered U of A's football team with an almost religious loyalty. For small children, Conway was a haven.

Wynne was the polar opposite of my slice of heaven. It was filled with mosquitoes and populated by rednecks for a lack of a better word. Even the humidity seemed thicker there.

I did manage to acquire a group of friends, mainly buddies with similar music interests. However, music wasn't just music in those days. It was the Beatles, the Moody Blues, and Dave Clark Five. Janis Joplin appeared. The Rolling Stones had already toured several times. The Doors were establishing themselves in music history. Music wasn't just music.

I entered eighth grade, and the world seemed paradoxically brighter yet darker. It was a time of political unrest. Dr. Martin Luther King, Jr. was killed 35 miles away. I still remember looking out the window at school, even though we were supposed to be under our desks. Rocks and bricks were being thrown through our classroom windows. Being the curious kid that I was, I naturally disobeyed my teacher and wanted to see why these objects were being hurled at our school and by whom. I was shocked to see friends trying to kill friends because of their color. Racial tensions exploded following the assassination of Dr. King. The otherwise peaceful environment was interrupted with outbursts between kids who had never quarreled before.

It seemed as if half the country was on fire. Riots popped up everywhere, and the tension was so thick you could cut it with a knife. This was further compounded by the conflict in Vietnam spiraling out of control. My early childhood years of blissful ignorance were tarnished by these ugly manmade confrontations. As children we were taught right and wrong, us and them, black and white. Everything was dichotomized, and it was with this primitive thinking that we were expected to grasp these horrible scenarios. Initially, I accepted this; it was how life was…unfair.

I was at the ripe old age of twelve when I rejected that way of thinking. Robert Kennedy was assassinated and with him the last glimmer of hope that things were going to get any better disappeared to me. I would no longer conform to this way of thinking; I was changed forever. I would not pretend to be someone or something that I was uncomfortable with, nor would I adhere to the ignorant racial standards that had been established. That same curious kid wanted to see what was out there, and if rebelling was the only way, then so be it.

CHAPTER 3
Welcome to OZ

Still being the curious kid I was, and still naïve to the real world, even though at that time I thought I had it pegged, I was open to adventure. My childhood friend, Garry, took me on my first adventure. It would be an adventure that would again change my life forever. One day in the summer of 1968, with our thumbs outstretched on the side of US highway 64, we hitchhiked to Memphis, Tennessee for a concert.

"Take this. It'll make ya feel better." He pushed his open palm towards me. On it was a small, yellow, conical tablet, smaller than an aspirin. Up until that time, I had no experience with drugs of any sort; I didn't even drink. A bad eggnog experience the previous Christmas had led me to dislike alcohol of any sort. About that time, an old Chevy truck with rusted pea-green paint that had prematurely faded to a color similar to baby vomit, came sputtering down the road and pulled off.

"You boooys want a riiide?" The man's backwoods upbringing made his southern drawl much more apparent even to us, his fellow southerners. I quickly, without any further hesitation or thought to its affects, swallowed the tablet and chased after Garry who was halfway to the truck. It wasn't long after we jumped into that truck that the effects of the acid began to take hold with Garry. His random giggling outbursts made me aware of this fact. The friendly backwoods truck driver was the only ride we had to hitch all the way to Memphis. The man dropped us off several blocks away from the concert. The overwhelming environment of liberal thinking "hippies" must have scared the man from driving up to the concert hall.

"This good for you boooys?"

"Yessir!" We hurried and jumped from the truck into a world that I had no idea existed. By the time we arrived in Memphis, the "window pane" acid, as I found out it was called, was beginning to take affect with me. I began to think that the faded truck was the symbolic shuttle taking us from our small secluded and known world into a completely alien one, filled with long hair, tie-dyed shirts, women without bras, and some of them without any clothes. It was as if the rules that applied back home were unknown. The psychedelics and my pubescent-enhanced hormones combined for a surreal experience that kept a smile on my face and a hard-on in my pants. Brightly colored visuals danced across my LSD enhanced world. Everything seemed more than what it really was. Street lights were gigantic faucets that poured light into the atmosphere. The crowds that lined the sidewalk and the outskirts of the arena seemed organic, as if everyone was part of one massive body being sucked into the experience. We piled into the auditorium's north hall in downtown Memphis. We found ourselves in the middle of the crowd, slightly to the right of center stage. The multi-colored lights on the stage illuminated the crowd; my attention was uncontrollably stuck on those lights. I looked everywhere frantically trying to see everything, as if naturally I knew this would not last forever. I followed the dancing lights across the crowd, not knowing what else to do. My attention was diverted by a beautiful young woman in her early twenties. Her shirt was made of thin white silk, and it might as well have been see through. My eyes became fixated on her beautiful breasts, and being twelve I wasn't quite sure what to think, but I was thinking a lot.

My awkward staring stopped abruptly as all the lights in the auditorium went black. My heart jumped, and for a second I was afraid of the unknown. The crowd erupted and I looked towards the stage. A man, barely visible only by his silhouette, had appeared seemingly out of nowhere. He struck his first guitar chord and the crowd became electrified from the reverberations. It was Jimmy Hendrix, and he filled the auditorium with the sounds of "Foxy Lady" almost perfectly, on cue, with the beautiful white bloused woman to my left. The lights beamed from the stage and the air filled with a bombardment of expertly played electric guitar. I felt like I was truly part of the Age of Aquarius. I was carried away with this new music and the dancing-light visuals became one blurry memory of ecstasy.

 I am still not exactly sure how we made it home that evening. It was almost like we floated home through the clouds, my senses overwhelmed and my young fragile mind over-exposed to this new culture.

 I returned home, my eyes now open to another world. My perspective was forever changed by that psychedelic night in Memphis, Tennessee.

 In an instant, my old world rushed into my colorful dreams of the concert. I sat up quickly, the daylight stinging my eyes, and my face was hot from the heavy-handed slap from my father. You see, back then parents could beat the shit out of the kids and not much was done about it. My sister, Marsha, got the worst, but I remember being beat many times until blood was running down my legs.

 "Where the hell were you last night!?" my father screamed. Veins pulsing in his temples, his piercing stare paralyzed me with fear. He slapped me again. The sound of smacking flesh awoke Garry.

 He pleaded with my father, as he struggled to open his eyes. "Mr. Shaw, please stop!" At that moment my father stopped his assault.

 "Alright, Garry," he said, and he quickly walked out without further words.

 These strict punishments were common in a household that embraced rural southern tradition mixed with old Scottish values. Children were raised with a healthy mixture of fear and brutality under an unwavering iron fist. My father was quick to start and end punishment, doing as much or as little as necessary to keep me submissive and in fear. He was a small man, only around five feet eight inches tall, but with a large presence. Some may have attributed this to a Napoleon complex, but I knew that it ran deeper than that, stretching back to his own upbringing.

Garry adapted to witnessing these scenarios, and he pretended as well as he could that he was not uncomfortable or affected by it. I was going to rebel; I was going to rebel all the way.

My mother had more fire being full-blood Scottish. Also quick to give out her own type of punishment, she would embarrass me by grabbing me, pulling my pants down and whipping me in front of my friends. She would chase me around the house with a broom that had a metal plate on it. If she couldn't catch me, she would hit me over the head with it.

It was even worse for Marsha, and she was getting more and more unable to take it. By the time she was a teenager, my father was against everything she did. One time she was picking me up from school, and she started going off about Dad. She was yelling that he couldn't treat her the way he did, and just at that moment the steering wheel came off the car! We both were in shock, yelling and scared to death. The car came to a stop in a ditch across from the school. We paused to take a deep breath thanking God we were still alive. Then, every word out of my sister's mouth had a condescending tone about my father and what he might do.

That night, at the supper table, my father and my sister got into it. It didn't help things that her nickname was "Easy".

Thinking I might help her out, and being 13, naïve, and immature, I asked her, "Well, why does everyone call you Easy?" I couldn't understand her rage for asking a simple question.

She was dating the guy next door. She ran across the street yelling, "I'm going to leave this family, and you all will never see me again!"

I took this statement to heart, because at this point in life I thought my sister was my best friend. About two weeks later, she got sick and didn't go to school. On about the fourth day of her missing school, I told my parents that she was obviously not sick, she was faking, and it wasn't fair that I had to go to school and she didn't. Marsha was three years, six months, and fourteen days older than me. Day after day, she just lay in bed, while I went to school.

My father and mother had never really told me the story about the birds and the bees. Apparently my sister was pregnant, and without anyone's knowledge, she and her boyfriend, Bill Goff, the boy next door, eloped to Tupelo, Mississippi.

I was unaware of any of this until one Saturday morning. I asked my mom and dad why my sister was gaining weight.

They replied, "Sit down son; we have something to tell you."

My mother became teary-eyed, and my father's face became red. Voices cracking, they said she was going to have a baby, and that she and Bill got married before telling us.

I cackled out loud because I thought it was a big joke. I turned around, about to walk out the door when Bill walked through the door and said hello to me, then turned and said, "Hi, Pop" to my father.

I felt like the melting wicked witch of the west in Wizard of Oz. I was melting emotionally, physically, and spiritually. Anyone who has been betrayed by a best friend would know this feeling. At this moment of my life I felt isolated and alone. I was dealing with emotions I never knew I had. It was as if God had pulled the rug out from under me; as if I was an outcast in my own home.

Marsha and Bill moved to Conway, and my niece was born. Damn! I was an uncle. I was jumping for joy. I traveled from Wynne to see my sister and get a look at my first niece. Marsha, being one of those over-protective mothers, knew I had strep throat.

As I stood tall and proud on the doorstep waiting to see my niece, the door opened and Marsha began screaming, "Don't bring him around my little baby!" Those words were a knife piercing my heart. I could not understand why Marsha was so angry at me. My parents tried to tell me it would be okay, but to a 14-year-old kid, it was like someone had shot me in the back.

The world around me seemed surreal. It was a very confusing time for a young boy. The war, riots, and racism was all that we ever saw on TV. Hope was just an afterthought.

CHAPTER 4
High School in the Seventies

My father got a new job in Jacksonville, Arkansas. I thought God had answered my prayers, delivering me from hell back to the real world again. Jacksonville was a crazy place in 1971. Everyone was either doing drugs, or riding Harleys, or both. For me it was just what the doctor ordered. I wasn't Marsha's little brother or Jr. anymore. I became my own person. Music became bigger than life. I would go to concerts to hear groups like Yes, Elton John, Little Feat, ZZ Top and the big time local band Black Oak Arkansas. I still remember seeing the Eagles as the backup band to Joe Walsh and Black Oak.

We all enjoyed freedoms back then like skinny dipping, sex, and of course music and drugs. My parents didn't like the way I was living, and the more they pushed, the more I pushed back.

It was a very exciting time for me, but it was also the beginning of a dangerous time. The war in Vietnam was getting closer to home, and people I knew were coming home either crazy, wounded, or in a box. Nixon was president, and it was also the time when a poll was out reporting that 92% of the student body of Jacksonville High School was doing LSD on a weekly basis.

I could go on a date with ten dollars. I could see a movie, eat a good meal, and get laid and come home with change left. My friends and I were into everything we could get into.

I remember one day some friends and I skipped school to see what trouble we could stir up. Of course, we meant no harm; we were just trying to have fun. I didn't know that a couple of my so-called friends had other plans. We went to the mall and hung out for awhile. When we decided we'd had enough of that, we headed to the car to leave. Just before we started the car, a couple of my friends wanted to go back in the mall to get a cassette tape. My friend, Lloyd, and I sat in my car while the others went inside. It seemed like it was taking a long time, so Lloyd and I went inside the mall to see what was going on. We got a feeling that we were being followed. Lloyd said he thought something was wrong, and he thought it would be better if we just went back to the car. At that moment two men stopped us and asked if we owned the silver 1963 Galaxy 500 outside. I told them it belonged to me, and they said they were the police, and we were in trouble for shoplifting. They arrested us.

Scared to death we told them we were just waiting for our friends, and we didn't know anything about any shoplifting. The cops said we were lying, and we were handcuffed and pushed into a cop car. Lloyd asked me what the hell was going on, because he knew we didn't do anything. I told him I didn't know.

The cop asked if he could search my car. Thinking that there was nothing to hide I said okay. It was awhile before he finished searching my car, and to our surprise he came back over to the police car holding a bottle of rum in his hand. All I could think of was that I was in deep shit, not only from the cops, but from my dad. I knew he was going to kill me when he found out. The cops proceeded to paint a picture of what our friends, or should I say our so-called friends, had been doing. They had stolen things from every store we went to that afternoon. For the first time in my life I knew was in deep shit, with no way out of the trouble I was in.

You see, in those days there wasn't probation; there was the one day wonder program. The judge said we boys were in for a treat, and we were sent to Cummin's Prison to work the fields with murderers, rapist, and the dregs of the world. At 5:00 in the morning, we were handcuffed to ten prisoners and led to the fields. The main guard was around 350 pounds of just plain meanness. There were four more guards with him. The big one rode a horse and marched us into a soybean field. He yelled at us, called us maggots, unchained us, turned around, and with big pointed boots he kicked me as hard as he could in the nuts. I saw stars, and felt unbelievable pain, and for the next 12 hours I was told by the prisoners that they were going to cut my fucking neck, and then go and fuck my mother until she screamed for more. It was the worst day of my life! I never wanted to end up in a place like that again.

CHAPTER 5
Senior Year...Caught Again

    So I was on to my senior year in high school. I was wearing big bell-bottom pants and t-shirts with peace signs on them. Even after the prison experience, we continued to stay fucked up. We'd get high and even higher. I remember taking my midterms doing acid. About two weeks into my senior year, I was in the bathroom at school before class one morning. A friend of mine walked in and asked me if I had any pot with me. I told him I only had a couple of joints, but if he had forty cents for lunch money, then I'd give them to him. We made the deal, but I didn't know there was another guy in a stall that saw it all.
    Five periods later I was in speech class when the vice principal came in. To myself I said shit; I hope he's not looking for me. And at that moment, he asked for me. I was holding a bag with me. All the way to the office he kept asking me if I had anything to tell him. I said no, but he kept asking me anyway.

When we got to the office, there was another kid there. Evidently, it was the kid in the stall. He pointed at me and yelled, "That's him! I swear! That's him!"

So they made an example out of me by handcuffing me and marching me through the locker area between classes. It was quite a scene. I was expelled from school until my court date. For the first time in a long time, I felt out of place and hatred filled my mind.

You see, in those days being found with pot was enough, but pot with the intent to sell was a max of 21 years in jail. All I could see was that guard, and that ugly motherfucker that wanted to cut my throat. Besides that, the first and only time I ended up in Cummins, my dad beat the living shit out of me when I got home.

It was three long weeks until court. At court, I stood by my dad as the judge said it was time to make an example of me. I cringed at the thought of being sent to prison again. To my relief, the judge sentenced me to a $1000 fine and one year probation. The next day, I would find out that I was to be home by 9:00 every night, and I also had to write a diary of what I did every day.

I was very cocky at that time in my life, so the first week I wrote that at 8:00 on Tuesday I took a shit. They didn't think that was funny. I was being watched very closely. One mistake, and I was in big trouble. Of course, my friends were staying as far away from me as possible.

The worst thing of all was that this experience would change my thoughts of man's worship of God. In my younger days I was into church and God. But now part of my sentence was to go to the First Baptist Church in Jacksonville both Wednesday and Sunday, escorted by two policemen. They picked me up at my house, and then they waited for the services to end and took me back home. The minister looked straight at me every time he mentioned the devil. Again I felt isolated, and after five months of this, not only was I going out of my mind at times, but my social life came to a stand still. In addition, my parents ignored me.

Since I had nothing else to do, I turned to my art. In the sixth grade I had shown my artistic talent where drawing is concerned. I actually won the elementary state art contest that year. However, no one at home encouraged me from that point on. And for sure, a guy didn't do such as that during the teenage years running around with buddies, so I wasn't into it up to this point. But, since everyone was steering clear of me like the plague, and I couldn't do anything else, I decided to begin drawing again. I had forgotten how much I enjoyed it and how good I was at it.

The one person who told me that I was special was my art teacher, and I couldn't believe it because I was so unaccustomed to any sort of praise. As a result, in my senior year I really got into drawing, and my drawings were a reflection of my life as I saw it. Acid gave me the avenue to see things that I had always taken for granted. Hands, trees, clouds, things that we all see every day became as statues upon a blue sky, or a green field. It was my way of breaking away from the angry world that was all around me.

This way of being was also was present in the clothes I wore, and the things I was into. Watergate, the war, it didn't matter. Nothing mattered. All I had to do was to look into the faces of my classmates and I could pretty much tell who was going places and who wasn't. I also think that shades of an addictive pattern were starting to show in me.

I was isolated in a different way. I wasn't the only one. Many of us were just scared, alone, and confused about the future for the first time in our lives. We were out of touch with the world around us simply because we were growing up and what was once the world's problems seemed now up to us to solve.

Many of us just said, "Fuck it!" It was as if we became a big bird with our heads in the sand hoping that we could run away and and when we came back everything would be okay. We had lost our trust in the country and our leaders, and we became part of the problem, not the solution.

We fell for everything, and didn't stand for anything. I remember walking outside one morning and my good friend Garry was asleep in his car. When I woke him, I asked him what he was doing. He said he ran away from home because his parents were getting a divorce. No one could seem to get a handle on anything, and there were no real answers on how to stop the snowball from rolling down the hill. So we just turned to the things that were everywhere; drugs, sex, and rock and roll.

After my probation, I took a trip to Conway to see my sister and some friends from my childhood. My sister was just about to have her second baby. I was tripping, walking down the street buck naked at four in the morning. I knocked on my sister's door and my brother-in-law answered. He asked what the hell I thought I was doing. The only answer I could give was that I was star gazing in the ruff. I was out of control for awhile, maybe because of feeling free now. Whatever the reason, I wasn't myself.

Some friends of mine, along with my parents told me it was time to think about college. I always wanted to go to the University of Arkansas, but as always, I was clouded by the drugs and a total lack of confidence. The thought of being told no was controlling my desire to succeed. Even when my art teacher said that she had sent my portfolio to some major colleges, I didn't believe in myself enough to trust my ability. So I went ahead and pre-enrolled at State College if Arkansas, which was one of the colleges in Conway. It was a surprise to me when they accepted me.

In many ways I settled for less. One would think that we were just young kids who didn't do anything but bitch about everything, instead of doing something about it. In a way that was true, but on the other hand, unless your family was rich you had to work for what you had. And I did. During this time of discontent, I worked two jobs. I think many of us did that. Even while we were working hard, I thought our government had different ideas of what the American dream was, and small town USA was being left behind; not from a lack of hard work, but from the lack of caring about its own people.

We as a nation, I truly believed, had lost our edge, not only within ourselves, but as a nation. As my dad always said, and still does, we didn't plan to fail. We just failed to plan. I still see this in the faces of the kids today. The same look is in their faces. They have the same type of problems without any hope of solving them. For myself I always thought that everything was going to be okay, and I would wake up to a bright sunny, day. It was just another way to put off until tomorrow what I could be doing today.

Graduation was coming up, and we were off to see the wizard. Young adults, both guys and girls, were getting their tuxes and dresses for the party of the century. We didn't know what the future held and really couldn't care less. I couldn't think that far ahead. Graduating was just a call to celebrate. For some, it meant going to work at the local factory like their fathers before them. For some it meant bright days ahead full of hope. And for the rest of us, well, we really thought the party would never end. We couldn't see that we were full of shit. No goals, no solutions, no drive to succeed. Just living. Trapped by our way of thinking. We didn't see what was coming. We truly couldn't see the forest for the trees. We did have a good time that night. I yelled out over the microphone during graduation, "Let's Party!" Then three days later I was driving my car to summer school in college. Neverland was about to begin.

CHAPTER 6
Neverland

NEVERLAND lasted through my college years and two years thereafter. Well, how does one get into and out of the twisted world we weave for ourselves? That's a good question. For me, it was like knowing about a trap before I was in it. The joke was on me. College, or the lure of it, was the trap and like quicksand one needs help to find a way out. For many, the summer of 1973 was a time of pure enjoyment. I did well in school. I felt a sense of confidence. I made Bs in all my classes. And the women; boy the women! I let my hair grow out, and the women were all around me and taking notice. Shit! I thought I was in heaven. I got laid all the time, and I had my eyes on them all. I became close to my childhood friends again. It was a great time to be young. There were parties all the time, and I thought I had it made. The living was easy. But that was the trap that many of us fell into.

 The only thing that saved me at the time was the fact that I was still living at home in Jacksonville with my parents. When I was just about to start fall semester, my parents decided to move back to

Conway. My dad got a better job as president of a company overseeing about 15 places like the one he had in Jacksonville.

At school, I thought I'd major in art, not only because I was drawing all the time, but because the college art teacher told me I was good at it. I was, for the first time, beginning to believe in myself. The semester started just before my parents got completely moved back to Conway, so I moved into the dorm. It was as if I had moved into a three story motel being run by Alice Cooper. It was a crazy place and a crazy time.

I had, by this time started seeing a girl from Conway named Cathy. Her parents were long time friends of my parents. Cathy was still in high school, but I liked her. I also became buddies with some frat guys, and I met a guy whose brother was a chemist at University of California. He sent us one hundred thousand sheets of "window pane" every two weeks, and we were selling it like hotcakes.

I was on top of the world. Instead of doing what I was supposed to do, like going to class, I was majoring in campusology, not art. Oh, I went to my art classes. I even took one hour courses on how to read a newspaper, bowling, and golf along with the classes that I needed to take. I took the sure thing classes to make sure that my grade average was 2.75 at the end of that first semester. But I was really just sliding by. I went from making money selling drugs, to playing spades in the student union, to pussy. Not what I would recommend to graduate, but what I wanted to do to stay on top.

Life for a young, naive, out-of-control kid was perfect, or at least I thought it was. I was throwing my life away, and didn't know it because I was stuck on stupid. My behavioral thought pattern was off the chart. I wasn't a student trying to study in any way, shape or form. I wasn't doing anything associated with school. I was just the life of the party. If I couldn't find a party to go to, I'd start my own just to fit in somehow.

The choices I made at this time became a problem as I got older. I was still that same, scared little boy on that ferry in Turkey. I had an internal conflict I battled with my whole life.

By the start of the spring semester, my grades were falling, and I was seeing Cathy more. I was also constantly hanging around a group of childhood friends. Some were still in high school and some of us were in college. What a crew we were! We did anything we wanted to do.

That year in Conway we saw Lynard Skynard, ZZ Top, Reo, and Styx for a dollar a concert. We were more blessed than we ever knew at the time. We were as crazy as they come. We would take frat brothers, tie them up and drive to places like Knoxville, Tennessee 450 miles away. We would strip their clothes off, leave them in a phone booth, pitch them a dime and tell them to call home for a ride. We would be so fucked up that the people we did that to would beat us home and pull the same pranks on us.

One time, with help from some of the guys, I got a guy high and left him in his room. A few minutes later the same guy was crawling down the hallway in the dorm. I yelled to the other guys to take a look! While the guy crawled hopelessly through the hall, we went to the store and got some Pepto Bismol and three bottles of super glue. I made him down the Pepto, and then I poured the super glue up the crack of his ass and wrapped him up with gray duct tape. I drove by the hospital, and at about 30 miles an hour I threw him out and drove off. Today we would be put in jail or worse. Back then it was just a prank.

My friends and I would sit around and smoke joints, do some cross tops and rjs, and talk about what was going on in the world and what was bothering us. We'd wait for the mushroom tea to cook and go get our ladies. Then we'd trip for 14 hours. Two days later we'd do it all over again.

But all was not well in Neverland. We were discontent with our lives. We didn't know why. We would sit and talk about getting away, but we didn't know where we wanted to go or how to get there. Our lack of action had us to the point of confusion. We just weren't happy.

I had to drop out of school at this point, and I went to work for my dad's company. That took me all over the state, but I still kept in touch with the gang constantly; and Cathy, too. I believe that the talks with my guys, my feelings for Cathy, and the job I had were having a positive effect on me.

A short time later I moved to a small town in northeast Arkansas. I was based there working for my dad, but I still traveled to many different places on the job. That got my mind in a better place, but I wasn't out of the woods yet.

I would meet up with Cathy, who at this point had started college at the University of Arkansas. In many ways I was envious of the fact that she went there and I didn't. But the trap was in place there for her as well.

The world's problems seemed to be calming down for the public, unless you were personally involved in them. Nixon was gone, and Ford was president. The war was almost over, but we still saw the retreat from Vietnam on the TV.

Closer to home, kids like myself were just glad that they weren't going over there. The life we were living just a year or so back seemed like a dream of sorts. Often there was a festival to enjoy. It was 1975 by then, and we still had our party times every week or two. We just did not have as many of them.

During this time, I reflected on the previous few years. I remembered some funny times and some not so funny times that would be everlasting memories. One such memory was the time my mother came into my room, and I was taking a shower. She told me my dad wanted to show me something. I got out of the shower, looked outside and saw him chopping up my tennis shoes with an axe. He was disgusted with their smell. He gave me money and demanded that I go buy some new ones.

One day, our gang got together at our regular place. We came to the conclusion that we all should join the Navy. We knew that if we did not do something, we were going to get busted, or worse. We also contemplated the friends we had lost. Friends who shot themselves, friends who had died in car or motorcycle wrecks, and one beautiful girl that we all had known since grade school who had accidently fallen off a cliff along the river and died. We wondered how and why we had survived it all! How did we end up being the ones on our way to breaking away from the trap of our past? Could we tap our heels together and get away to where we needed to be, or would we just sit and have life slide by?

I was becoming weary of the life I was living. You see, three of my friends had joined the navy by this time. I was still working for my dad's company. I told my dad I wanted to join the Navy. He responded by telling me that if I joined the Navy, he would have my nuts on a platter, and that if I wanted to join anything it would be the Air Force. He also told me that I should consider my mother's feelings. It would break her heart because her dad had died in World War II in a prisoner of war camp in Germany. What they didn't know was that I had already had my physical.

I just had to get out of there. At that time, I had started working in Little Rock at a nursing home. It was a terrible place. The owner was a drunk, and the patients were in bad shape. One of the vice-presidents of the company was there, and he just stood around like his shit didn't stink, while the rest of us worked our asses off 22 hours a day.

So, one morning I had enough of this asshole telling everyone what to do. In my opinion, he didn't know a damn thing. I grabbed my rag I was using and threw it in his face. I yelled at him. I asked why he didn't get to work, too. Mad as fire, he went to the owner, who happened to be talking to my dad at the time. He said he was going to have to fire me. He told them what I had done. To my surprise the owner said that he thought I was right. He told the vice-president to go home and get some work clothes on, or don't come back and he would send him his paycheck. Motherfucker, I thought to myself. I didn't get fired. But, I was always on edge like that.

The owner of the nursing home told my dad that he thought it was time for them to consider putting me in the administrator-in-training program. We had just opened another facility in Batesville, Arkansas, so I started working there. And, without my parents' knowledge, I joined the Air Force on the delayed enlistment plan.

It was 1976. America was two hundred years old. Shit! In my opinion, we hadn't learned a thing from all this country had been through. America didn't care about their people's plight through those times. There was still rage and riots and lies from the powers that be, and doing the same things expecting different results is and always will be insane. As goes history, so go the memories of my life.

My grandfather was going into the hospital for a simple ulcer operation, and I wasn't too worried about it. My dad was. I guess he was scared for his dad.

I got a call while I was working in Batesville one day. It was my dad. He said, "I would like you to come home now."

"What's wrong, Dad?" I asked.

"It's Pop." That was what I called my grandfather. A sudden sense of fear came over me. The man that I thought was invincible was sicker than I knew. I drove as fast as I could to get to Little Rock. When I got there, my worst fears came true. Somehow they had a breakdown during the operation, and he developed a staph infection. They had to operate again.

I went back to Batesville to work, but I became nervous as to the outcome with Pop. This great man had to quit school after the sixth grade to help raise his brothers and sisters because his dad was badly hurt in a tornado when he was young. And we thought we had it bad. This mountain of a man worked his whole life for the greater good. God knew what he was doing when he made this man. Shoulders as wide as the Grand Canyon and character as good as you will ever find in a man; that was my Pop.

It was July when I got the call that I dreaded so much. In tears, and driving like a wild man, I got to the hospital just in time to see my dad crying as they lowered Pop's bed. I knew that life would never be the same. I had never been this near to death before. At the funeral as the family and Cathy looked on, I knew that Neverland was over, never to return again.

CHAPTER 7
Aim High! The Air Force Years…..Up, Up, and Away!

My Poppy had just died, and I knew it would be bad timing, but I had to tell my mom and dad that I had joined up. I was on my way home, two weeks after Pop's death, and trying to think of a way to tell them the truth. It became more apparent to just tell them. So, when I arrived home, I walked into the house and immediately I told my mom and dad to sit down. I had something that I had to say. I somehow felt that Dad knew what I was going to say.
"I joined the Air Force!"
Mom said, "What did you say?" Then she started to cry as she walked swiftly to their bedroom.
Dad just lowered his head and watched my mom disappear. He asked, "Why? You hear Mother crying."
I looked my dad in the eyes and said, "Dad, it's something I feel I have to do."
"Then you better explain that to her. Mothers all over the world do not want their sons to join. Especially when it's their only son."
After those words, I walked oh, so slowly to my mother's room. When I walked in, she was sitting on her bed just shaking her head.

I could only say to her, "Mom, I have to do this. I'm trapped here!"

Slowly she looked up at me and said, "Just come home to me, Son. Just come back home to me!"

"I will Mom. I will."

She got up and put her arms around me tightly and held me for awhile. It was a moment I will never forget. She asked if I had told Cathy yet. I hadn't, and it being summer, Cathy was at home.

I went over to her parents' house. It was an older home that was well kept, and like a lot of homes in the south, the tree limbs hung over the street shading the road. It had very pretty and very southern redish brick, and it was trimmed in white. I walked up to the side door as I had done many times before, this time more slowly, and rang the doorbell. It felt different this time. It was as if it were a stranger's house that I had never visited before. Maybe because of the reason I was here. I didn't know exactly why. It just felt foreign.

Cathy answered the door, jumped on me giving me a big kiss, and said, "You know I love you!"

"Yes, I do," I replied.

We went inside. Her mom and sister greeted me. I told them all to sit down. Before anyone could say anything, I told them I had joined the Air Force, and was to go to basic in September. An eerie silence filled the room. I explained that it was just something I had to do. I could see the tears starting to fill Cathy's eyes. I asked her not to cry and gave her a hug. Her mom asked if I had told my parents. As I was telling her I had, Cathy ran upstairs to her room. I moved to go after her, but her mom asked me to just let her go. She said Cathy was a girl in love and very emotional.

I left her house. As I drove home I said a little prayer, and asked God to help me out on this one. Well, I guess He did, but not the way I thought He would. I got home, and I could still hear my mom crying. I felt that I had hurt her deeply, but I guess it was like every mom when they get the news of their boys going away to join the service. At that time I asked God to watch over her because she was one of a kind, but He knew that already.

The next sixty days zoomed by and before I knew it, it was time for me to go. I said my goodbyes to my friends and family. Mom, Dad, and Cathy drove me to the Little Rock Airport. I was a little scared because I had never flown by myself before. I was nervous as

I got on the plane. All kind of thoughts went through my mind. As the plane took off, I could see my parents waving goodbye at the end of the runway, and I felt a little bit of uncertainty. The flight went to Dallas, then on to San Antonio, and then I rode a bus to the base. When I got there it was like I had been dropped off in a different country.

Boy! Was I in for a treat! The guys that were on the bus with me were the ones that I would go through basic with, and I believe that none of us knew what to expect. But we found out shortly after that. We were standing right by the bus, when all of a sudden I heard, "Click, click, click! Pick up those bags you maggots! Move!!! I said move, maggots!!"

As we looked around I couldn't make out who was talking to us, and the two guys that were beside me asked me if that was a woman's voice or… and at that same time, out of the shadows appeared a woman, I think. I told the guys next to me that I thought it was a woman.

"Jesus! I said move!" We looked at each other and wondered who she was talking to. She was about 5 feet something, but her voice sounded as if she was 10 feet tall. She looked my way, and looking me right in the eyes she repeated, "Jesus! I said your name right, boy?"

"No, Ma'am!"

"You look more like Jesus than anybody else in this group!"

"No sir!"

"What did you call me? Stand at attention, Jesus!"

"Yes Ma'am, Sir!"

"What? Jesus, are you blind, boy?"

"No, Ma'am!"

"You must be, boy! It's to you, Jesus!"

"Yes Ma'am. Sergeant, Ma'am."

The guy beside me started to laugh, and she said, "Are you laughing at me, boy?"

"No Ma'am," he said.

"You can laugh over there, and while you're at it give me 20!"

"Yes, Ma'am!" he said. So the guy went over to where she pointed, but it wasn't far enough to suit her.

"I said over there, boy!" He kept walking and all at once he fell, face first into a ditch.

The other sergeant, who was a man, said to the guy in the ditch, "I'm going to have you butt fucked for nine weeks, boy. You're going to think I'm your mama before you are finished. Now move!"

At the same time, the lady sergeant, and I use that term lightly, said to me, "Jesus!"

"Yes, Ma'am, Sergeant, Sir!"

"We are going to make you pretty tomorrow!"

"Yes, Ma'am," I answered.

They had us run up three flights of stairs to our barracks, where our home would be for the next nine weeks. As they yelled at all of us, I thought to myself, "God, I'm in hell. Please let me wake up from this fucked-up dream."

My father's bitching at me for most of my life and telling me that that I will never amount to anything really prepared me for this very thing. And at the time, I didn't even know it. Shit! I'm not in Kansas anymore.

At four o'clock sharp the next morning, they woke us up yelling at us the whole time, even turning over lockers of some of the guys. At least I knew that I didn't need to do anything until they told us to. We were to go down to the yard and stand at attention. The next few hours would prove to be my worst during basic. They took us through the welfare line, as I called it, to get our socks, shoes, and new clothes. I came to hate green with a passion after that day. The worst thing was that the sergeant noticed that I had the longest hair in the platoon. She told the barber to make my haircut a special one. It took four years to grow, but it took them less than four seconds to cut it off my head.

I thought the barber was finished with me, and I started to get up when the sergeant said, "Jesus, aren't you forgetting something?"

"I don't think so, Sergeant."

"Are you blind and deaf, boy?" she asked.

"No, sir!" I said.

She yelled at me, "I think you are, boy. And if I ever hear you call me sir again, then I'll send you home in a box. Do you hear me, boy?"

"Yes, Sergeant!"

That's when she turned to the barber and said, "Put Jesus' hair in a box." And then turned back to me and said, "Jesus, you will carry that box until you die, or until I say to throw it away. Do you understand me, boy?"

"Yes, Sergeant."

"Now move, boy."

"Yes, Sergeant!"

I grabbed the box with my hair in it and went outside the barber shop. Things got worse. I had to march with my hair in that box for three days. I don't think I ever felt more foolish in my life. We lost five guys that first day. I guess they thought that this would be a piece of cake. Well, it was not.

My hair was so short that when I laid my head on my pillow, it pinched my head. The one good thing that day was that having worked in a nursing home, I was good at making a bed. So when I made my bed, hospital corners of course, I made it so that I could slide out of it, tighten it, and slide back in it. I didn't have to make it again while I was in basic.

It wasn't long until I noticed that the guys who smoked got to take a break to smoke after every meal. So as soon as we were allowed to go to the PX, I got a carton of cigs so I wouldn't have to stand at attention for forty to forty-five minutes. Later that came to be a bad choice.

The rest of basic was going to classes and marching. Yes, I shot perfect at the shooting range, and yes, I got to wear my little ribbon. Other than that, I just had to have the ability to put up with the bullshit, and the running, and the marching; running and marching. When we had time to fool around, we had some fun. But we didn't get to do that much.

We were playing football one day, and I broke my finger. Now, I wasn't smart enough to go to the hospital, and a funny thing happened. A coreman saw it and took a coat hanger and bent it around my finger, then wrapped gauze around it. Well, that was fine and good. I knew that if I could put up with it for six months, then it was the Air Force's problem.

By this time we were down to about 26 of us. We started with 39. A lot of the guys quit, and the ones that did not want to get out had to start all over. That was just the way it was. I guess some people just aren't made for the service, and some are. By the time we had our qualifying run, which is running a mile and a half in 12 minutes, there were about four who had to start over because they couldn't run it fast enough.

It was time for our family to come see what we had become, and how we looked. I saw my mother and dad, and the first thing out of my mom's mouth was, "I can see your ears. A.J. And you do have eyebrows."

I felt for the first time in my life that I accomplished something, not only for myself, but by myself. I knew that basic wasn't over yet, but I knew now that I was going to make it. We got our pictures taken, and we were looked up to, and it was all worth it.

CHAPTER 8
Aim High! The Next Step!

    I really can't remember the date, but we all said our goodbyes to the guys who were off to their next station while the rest of us went to ours. I thought hell, they flew us down here, and being the Air Force they would fly us to the next step of our training. But I was wrong. About 4:00 in the morning we were rushed outside and loaded into a bus.
    I said, "What! A bus! You have to be kidding me."
    I still remember that damn bus ride. Our company's airmen weren't the only ones on the bus. All of us were cramped into a bus that should have had maybe 50 people on it, but I think there were about a hundred of us, or it seemed to be.
    As we rode, I was kind of in a mood. I was remembering when, on the 29th day of basic training the drill sergeant called me Jesus and told me to report to the first sergeant's office. Hell, I thought, what did I do? I had a lot of things going through my mind, but I knew I hadn't done anything wrong. But I didn't know what was going on.
    When I arrived, I was informed that the guaranteed job that I was to have, in fact, wasn't guaranteed anymore. The first sergeant told

me that I could get out if I wanted. I told him I would gladly take my second choice. He was satisfied and he dismissed me, and I thanked him. So here I was, going for my second choice.

We were headed to Mississippi. Shit! What the hell! I hate Mississippi! I hate this fucking bus. It took about 14 hours to get to Keesler Air Force Base. I thought I was somewhere between the KKK, a swamp, and the Gulf of Mexico. And I was right, too. I was in Mississippi! Shit! It was a sight to behold! They had one bar and one little shopping center. I remembered when I lived in Wynne and we read where Hurricane Camille came right through the area where I was now. I wondered if it was even safe to be here.

About that time a C-130 flew over, and I knew I was where I wanted to be. A base is its own city within a city, with its own ways, its own rules, and its own punishments. For a young kid from small town USA, it was very exciting. As I got to my room in the barracks, there were guys and girls from all over the country. I was truly happy for the first time in a long time.

The next day we started training. At first it was hard, and then it became second nature to me. The math part was a little harder than I thought it would be, maybe because I never was good at taking tests, or maybe because I hadn't taken one lately without the influence of some kind of drugs. I also was in fear of getting kicked out of the Air Force. It seemed that I was the only one that was having trouble.

I remember the time they gave us the swine flu shot. I was scared. Hell, after the lines of shots we had to go through in basic, it's no wonder we were scared to death. It was about seven thirty in the morning when I got my shot, and by 9:00 I was getting sick. I thought I was going to get to go back to the barracks, but the instructor wouldn't let me go. I was too young to understand what the hell he was thinking. I thought it was shitty to let a student get sick in his class, and not be allowed to even go to the doc. The other students could see that I was ill. By noon, I was running a 102* temp, and it was pouring down rain. To this day I don't know how I could even breathe.

When class was over the rain was worse, and it was about a mile to the barracks. I was trying the best I could to get there, but I was in bad shape. I finally made it and went straight to my room. My fever was almost 106* when it finally broke about 9:00 that night. I surely thought I was going to die that day, but God was on my side I guess.

My friend from a small town about 40 miles away stayed with me. He was a good guy.

About a week later all the guys that had been in for a while started to taunt us newbies about where we were going to be stationed.

They would shout, "Hey! They are going to send you guys to Why Not Minot, South Dakota." Then they would laugh and go away.

Well, it came time for our orders to come in, and I was excited and nervous at the same time. I was called, and to my surprise I was to report to the 3625th squadron at Tyndall A. F. B. in Panama City, Florida. That made me the happiest guy in town. I felt like I had won the football pool or something. I had three weeks to report.

I was able to go home during the holidays, and on the drive home I had a lot of time to think. Many things were going through my head like what would it be like at Panama City, and what job would I be doing. I was excited all the way around. I felt good about myself. I was in some shape or form going to finally do what I was trained to do.

I was somewhere in Mississippi, almost to the state line, when I turned on the radio, and to my surprise I heard Pat Travers and Beaker Street on KAAY. KAAY was a radio station in Little Rock that I could pick up just about anywhere in the states, and it played the best music; all rock and roll, and I mean the good stuff. It was harmony to my ears, and it was just what the doctor ordered.

When I got into Arkansas I felt as if I could float home. It felt like freedom. It was around midnight as I pulled into Conway. I was home! When I arrived at my parents' house, I saw a new car in the driveway. Another new car. It must be nice.

My mom was waiting up for me. She gave me a big hug and said, "I love you son. It's good to have you home."

Boy did it feel good to sleep in my bed again. But, I felt a little out of place. I knew I was becoming the man I wanted to be. I was thinking of the future. Being a little restless, I went outside to smoke a cigarette.

I saw my mother in her greenhouse doing the same.

"Is Dad's snoring keeping you up? I asked her.

"That man is going to have to buy me a house with a bedroom for him, or add on to this one," she replied. "What are you doing smoking?"

"I didn't want to stand at attention while the guys who smoked got a break after chow."

She gave me another hug and said, "Well baby, you're growing up too fast for a mother."

"I love you too, Mom." We had a good talk and then went to bed.

The next morning I was just getting up and around and my dad asked me what I thought of his new car. I asked him what he needed with a new car. He and Mom had a car. He just answered with, "Yes, we do."

Cathy was home from school and we had a good holiday season. By this time, she had transferred to a school in Arlington, Texas. I supposed we were going our different ways.

It seemed that the three weeks were over before I knew it. About the time I was almost ready to leave, my dad told me he was proud of me, and threw me the keys to the new car. I was surprised and asked him what those were for. He told me that he bought the car for me! I was at a loss for words. I gave him a hug and told him and my mom that I loved them and would not let them down.

Cathy was crying and did not want me to go, but I told her that I go where the Air Force tells me to go. I told her that I loved her.

I still was overwhelmed by the new car. It was the first time that I had ever gotten anything like that. I, along with many people my age never knew that feeling.

I was on my way. The drive was not only full of hope, it was full of excitement. I was driving a new car. Damn! It was so hard to get it through my head that it was mine.

I got to the border between Alabama and Florida. It was a beautiful day. The sun was shining. It was as if it was shining just for me. My dad and I had looked over the map. I knew to get on Highway 98. The beach and blue-green water was so pretty that I started to slow down.

I passed a beautiful woman walking along the beach. I took a double take. It looked like Marla. Hell! It was her! It was a girl I dated once. She was with her best friend. They had moved down to this area. I sure didn't expect to see them! I turned around and yelled, "Hey! Girl!"

She looked, then looked again and said, "A.J.! Is that you?"

I said, "In the flesh." I got out of my car, and we gave each other a big hug.

"What are you doing here, and what happened to your hair?" Marla asked.

I told her about joining the Air Force, and I told her I was stationed in Panama City. She remembered my friends and me talking about joining the Navy. I told her my friends had joined the Navy, but my dad said he would have my balls if I joined anything but the Air Force. So, there I was.

"Well," she said. "It's good to see you. Let's go."

"Where?" I asked.

"To my place," she said.

So we went to their house. It was good to see a familiar face. We talked for awhile, said our goodbyes, then I was off to Panama City and Tyndall Air Force Base.

It was a beautiful 60 mile drive to Panama City from Destin. When I got to Panama City Beach, there were women everywhere! I thought I had landed in heaven. The beach was pretty fine. Well, saying fine isn't enough to describe it. Unbelievable would be a better way to put it. So, here I was in the middle of paradise.

I drove to the base. I was a little cautious because I really didn't know what I was in for. People who have been in the military know that the real training comes after tech school. It's all about on- the-job training, and I had not experienced that yet. I got to the gate, showed my ID, and asked where the 3625th squadron was. They told me how to get there, and also where the barracks were. As I drove through the base I was not thinking of this place as a temporary station, but as my home for as long as the Air Force wanted me to be here. It was as if I felt a part of it rather than just passing through. I think all new young airmen think that way.

I found my barracks pretty easily, parked and went inside. What was inside was troubling. To my surprise the first guy that said hello was a little guy named Denny, and we hit it off right away. He showed me my room. Denny was from Wisconsin, Spooner to be exact. Of course I didn't know where that was, but I could tell it must be a small town. It showed; he was a great guy.

As soon as I got settled he asked me if I smoked. I said yes because I thought he meant cigarettes. I soon found out that was not what he meant. He took me to a room where two guys from Ohio were. As he introduced me to J.J. and Jr., it was clear that Denny wasn't talking about cigarettes. The room was full of pot smoke, and it was like walking into a haven of smiles and hellos. About five guys were in there getting high. That was right up my alley. J.J. was from Columbus, and Jr. was from Sin City. They were both good guys, but the guy that threw the biggest shadow was Modo. One can only describe him as a big guy about six feet five inches tall and around 260 lbs. Modo was from Alabama, but his parents were from Robbins, Georgia. He was a real southerner, and the kind of guy that if you ever made a friend out of him, you had a friend for life. But, if he didn't like you, he would either beat the hell out of you or just shoot you with his 9mm Berretta. J.J. asked me if I wanted a hit off the joint.

"Hell, yeah! I do." So I took a big drag and before I knew it I was higher than Cooter Brown.

Jr. asked me if that was my new car out front, and all I could say was, "Yeaaahhh!" Matter of fact, that's all I could say for awhile.

J.J. gave Jr. a high five, then Modo gave both of them a high five. They all decided right then, that I was a winner. They started laughing and saying that I was fucked up.

I said, "Hell! I'm a Hog fan. Every good Hog fan knows how to get high."

Jr. said, "Hell! I like him already".

And that is how I finished the next step. The rest of the night was just a prelude to what would follow.

CHAPTER 9
Let's Get to Work…Now to Get to the Job at Hand!

I got to know everyone in the barracks, and all but a couple of them got high. Only a few knew what they were doing, though. It was apparent that the 35-10 was in effect at work.

I was introduced to the squadron's commander, the first sergeant, and my sergeant who was my real boss. He was a staff sergeant and a big asshole to boot, but he was one of those guys that had been in about 16 years and thought he knew what he was doing. But like everything else in life, there are people that think they know what they are doing, and then there are guys that know what they are doing. This guy knew just enough to get by, and that was just what he had been doing for as long as he had been in the Air Force; just enough to get by.

I met a couple of guys, tech sergeants, and they had been in combat. They also taught military aikido, which I didn't know. They were really bad sons-of-bitches. They taught me a lot, not only about fighting, but about the service.

I became pretty good at my job learning radar, and training officers how to do it. We worked only five and half hours a day, and had weekends off. We made good use of all that time off. It became apparent that all kinds of military officers from around the world were learning here, and we were the ones teaching them. In a way it was cool, but in a way I was thinking that maybe it wasn't a good thing to teach the things we knew to everyone. I was right, but that would play out later.

J.J. and Jr. were part of the crew we all hung around with, but it was Denny, Modo, and Larry that hung out together the most. My roommate and Denny and I took lessons from Sonny and Jim. They were the tech sergeants that taught us, and we all looked up to them. The rest of us went all over the place on weekends, and got high and got drunk all the time.

I remember the time the squadron CO came into the barracks to let us have some of his birthday cake. We were all passed out from playing the board game, *Passout*. But, instead of using cigarettes and beer, we used rum, pot, and mushroom tea. All of us were just motionless, without a clue. When he walked in we were all just too fucked up to care, and to me he looked like a bullfrog with big ears carrying purple cake. Well, let's just say it was indescribable.

Back then there were no drug tests, and no one cared anyway. That was the way it was. Oh, if he wanted to, he could have had us all thrown out of the Air Force. But, he just let us go. There were many times when we could have been busted out, but we weren't. As long as you did your job and kept your off time under wraps and stayed out of the way of the real trouble makers, the higher ups stayed out of your business.

I stayed busy. I was too busy to think about a lot. But, something was missing. I didn't know what, though. I was getting good at aikido, and it was time to break my first board. Seven or eight of us guys were in class and lined up to break boards. I was a little over confident, to say the least. When it was my turn, I did the wrong thing. I just hit it with my little finger. I didn't know what hurt worse, my finger or my head. Sonny hit me with I don't know what, and I ended up off the backboard 12 feet away. I never made that mistake again.

At work, I got the opportunity to move to the sage squadron across the street. That was where the real stuff was going on. I had been training officers with simulators. Across the street, we worked with live traffic. They showed me how to track live traffic, and I got to an unofficial skilled level. We were plotting and working with top secret materials. I really got to the point where I did not like working with butterballs, second lieutenants. They were the dumbest guys ever. They were college grads who didn't know their left from their right. How they ever got to be officers I'll never know.

Modo, Denny, and I partied a lot. We went to Tampa to see Pink Floyd and Zeppelin. We went to Atlanta and partied in The Underground. We went everywhere we could for a good concert or a good time. During all my off time, I was experiencing a lot, but I couldn't see what effect it was having on me. I was spending my time having a good time. As far as akido goes, I was missing a good lesson that Sonny and Jim were trying to teach me. That lesson was to find inner peace. It just went right over my head.

Jr. and J.J. were black, Pepe was Latino, and Modo and I were from the south. Denny and Larry were from the north, and Dave was from California. We didn't look at color. We were a group, and we had each other's back. All we saw were friends.

We were at the club on the base, and disco music was filling the night air. We all looked over and saw what we thought was the devil. We weren't ready to see that at all. What we saw was a guy in six inch heels. That was the end of it all, we thought. There was cocaine and bullshit.

The America that we grew up in was going fast. To us it was all about change. We, like many people at that time, just were not willing to change with it. But, we had no choice. Character didn't matter anymore. It was becoming the dark time, just ten years after Dr. King's death. Where was the world going?

That's when I called and asked Cathy what she thought about us getting married. That is what I thought was missing. It was the beginning of a series of bad choices that would cost me a lot of grief. I told Denny, Modo, and J.J. my plans. They thought I was crazy. I was stuck on stupid and would not listen to the people that I believed in the most.

One night, Sonny took us to a club that was on the beach. Jim said when you know the ability of the person that has done you wrong, you show him, not through words but by deeds. Sonny was 5 feet 4 inches tall, and maybe 130 lbs. He was a great man that had been to hell and come back to tell about it. Jim was 6 feet and 200 lbs., going bald and a little overweight. Jim told us to sit back and watch. Sonny walked inside this crazy "disco meets muscle" type of place. We did not like coming here, but that did not affect either one of these men, not at all. Jim said that one of the guys there called Sonny a "nigger"! Shit! Again, Jim told us to watch. These guys looked like they had an air hose blown up their asses. They were big and they thought they were bad. Sonny walked by and one of them pushed him down. We were ready to start a fight when Jim again insisted we just watch. Sonny got up and with his hand he motioned the biggest one to "come get you some". The guy came at Sonny and Sonny hit him hard and fast. He knocked him clean out with one punch. Then another one ran at him, and he had the same result. Jim was laughing out loud. He turned to us and told us to think about what we would do if put into a position like that. He told us to think what could happen if we were not ready for what life may bring. That meant that if the mind, body, and spirit are not in tune with each other, then evil will take over and goodness will be for naught.

    It was not long after, maybe three weeks, that we were at our favorite club. Jim had his big-ass shepherd dog, Sally. A similar thing happened. Sally did not move unless Jim told her to do so. She was a beautiful dog, but you somehow knew by her manner that you didn't want to mess with her either. Outside when Jim was saying goodnight to us, he turned and a 1978 Grand Prix hit him in the parking lot. The blow knocked him back. At first we thought it killed him. When he hit the gravel, he sprang right back up, and in one motion put his fist through the front window of the car, grabbed the guy driving by the throat, and calmly said, "Slow down." The guy in the car shit himself, and we almost did, too. I just cannot explain how we felt.

    I was at a crossroads with my feeling towards Cathy. My good friends were trying to tell me about her. They all said that they thought it would be a bad and stupid thing to marry her. I already had permission to go to Texas to get married, but all my friends told me to think it over. They did not want to see me hurt. I walked into Modo's room. J.J., Denny, and Dave said that they were worried about me. They thought it would be a good idea to take me somewhere.

    "Take me where?" I asked.

    Denny said they wanted to take me to a new mushroom field he had found. I was not myself, but I had always tried to keep my promises. I believed that people were found to be untrustworthy. Still the little boy on that ferry, scared and lonely, I would give into what was really the truth. I think they call that denial. So to their credit, Denny and Modo went on and headed for a field of dreams so to speak. It lasted all weekend for Modo, but would prove to be funny, shitty, and down right crazy for Denny and me.

First we went to find this so called "party" that Modo said was out in the woods north of the base, and before you knew it we were lost. It was getting dark by this time, and we were in the Lautermobile. That's what we called Denny's royal blue 1968 Mercury, draped in royal blue with blue dice and other wild get-up. So there we were lost in the woods and Denny being the short little guy he was could hardly see. Modo was saying turn here, and go here, and before we knew it Denny had run off the road and got stuck in the mud. Modo and I were used to this, but Denny was not. Dark and high is not the way you want to be stuck out in the middle of nowhere. We did not how much time had passed, but we couldn't get the car out. We kept seeing light from a distant but didn't know if it was someone's house or if the speed and pot were just playing tricks on us. Then, we saw lights heading toward us.

"Shit! It's the cops!" Modo shouted.

Denny was freaking out, and he threw his pot into the woods.

"Boys, what are you doing here?"

I answered, "Well officer, we took the wrong turn I think, and now we're stuck and don't know where we are."

"Let's see some ID, boys."

"Yes sir!" we said, and we pulled out our military IDs.

"Well boys, you need to find a way back to base because you are in range of some 80 year old moonshiners that think you are the feds trying to get them, and they called us."

Modo and I felt a little better when he said that. You see, in the south we are used to that from the local sheriff because all around the south the local law works with people like that just about all the time. It's more of an information exchange than anything. Plus, the cops get free booze.

So they left, and Denny was freaking out. "We're going to die!"

Modo started laughing and walked towards the end of the road. We couldn't see very well and Denny was not too pleased. He kept saying he was afraid that we were going to get killed.

I said, "Come on. No one is going to die. Come on, you better start walking."

So after Modo stopped laughing we still did not know where we were, and it was getting late. By the time we got to the road, a couple of assholes had stopped and pulled off the road. Modo just shot at them and they took off.

We finally made it back, but we were all in a bad mood. I was in the mood to just go to Texas and get married. We had the mushrooms, so Denny cooked them up. He told me to drink up and stop thinking about going and doing something I would regret. My thoughts were so far away from any kind of reality that I was not myself. It didn't take long for the tea to hit, and Denny did not want to leave me. All the guys were worried about me. But, I didn't see that I was in the danger zone. It all started a chain reaction that would last for two weeks.

I don't recommend that anybody do mushrooms for two weeks at a time, but Denny and I did. We were tripping at work, play, and everywhere in between. My jaws were hurting from laughing for so long so I took a couple of pain pills, and drank a fifth of tequila and that didn't even phase me. It was a miracle that I didn't have a bad trip, but that would change in a crazy way.

We were going to go after work to our favorite club. Modo wanted to go and trip with us, so away we went. It took about twenty or thirty minutes to get there, and we were tripping by the time we arrived. The club was packed and we were feeling pretty good about the way the night was going. We were there about twenty minutes when Denny said he had to go to the bathroom. I didn't really think anything about it, but when you are as high as we were lots of things are on your mind at the same time. Anyway, you don't think about simple things like going to the bathroom. That's when Modo wanted to leave, and he wanted me to tell Denny that we were going down the street so he could join us when he was finished in the bathroom. As I was on my way to tell Denny our plans, I picked up on an odor coming from the bathroom. When I opened the door, Denny was, to say the least, in somewhat of a situation. The look on his face said it all.

I said, "Dude, are you o.k.?"

He turned and looked at me in total agony.

"Say man, Modo has to go, so we will be right back."

He just looked up, and all he could say was, "Ohhh."

In the frame of mind I was in, I didn't take that seriously, either. I just thought it was something he ate. So Modo and I got into my car, and pulled out of the parking lot. Before I drove two hundred feet I started shitting uncontrollably. I was in shock.

Modo looked over at me and said, "What the hell!" He had a look of total disbelief.

I said, "I'm crapping all over myself for no reason." I pulled over got out and ran as fast as I could into the water, throwing my pants off as quickly as I could. I don't think the sharks would even try to mess with my pants. I had a trail of crap behind me, because I was still shitting as I ran back towards the car. I got as far as one of those big rocks that were painted in white that lined the beach. I jumped onto the rock still crapping all over it. I knew then why Denny looked the way he did when I opened the door to the bathroom.

In my moment of torment, Modo was shaking his head, and saying that I had brought him down. "You done brought me down!" he kept saying.

"I brought you down! Hell! At least you're not on top of this rock!"

All of a sudden bright lights hit me. All I could think of at that moment was, "Officer, I don't know. It maybe was something I ate." As I put my hands up to cover my eyes, I saw my hands on the jail cell bars and me saying, "I'm not guilty."

When I saw it was not the police, but an elderly lady in total shock over what she was seeing, I told Modo that we needed to get back to base.

"You ain't getting in this car!"

"Hell! It's my car! Anyway, look, Modo, I have stopped crapping, and I've got to get some clothes on."

After intense negotiations I convinced him to let me drive back to base. I'm sure we looked like something on Laugh-In! We got through the back gate and pulled up to the barracks. I ran in with Modo behind me still saying that I had brought him down. He sat in the TV room, and the guys were asking what the hell was going on. I said I was going to write a book about this shit, and Modo was going to just sit there because I had brought him down. I went to my room, got some clothes and a towel and soap and got into the shower. As I was cleaning myself up, I felt like I was starting to trip again! I was still high!

I walked into the TV room, and Modo was sitting there. He started to laugh, and so did I. We could not believe what we had just gone through. As we sat there I started to wonder if we had forgotten something. I guess about 45 minutes had gone by.

All at once we looked at each other and shouted, "Denny!"

He was still at the club! We drove back to the club and opened the door to see Denny on top of the bar with a rope around his neck.

We yelled, "No! Don't! He's tripping! And it's not his fault!"

"He clogged up the bathroom toilet!" everyone shouted. The women were mad, the band had to stop playing, and they were going to hang him.

"Heeellllp Meeeee!!!!" Denny cried.

So Modo got his 9mm out and said, "He is on mushrooms!" Then, we got him down.

He pushed Modo and said, "Where the hell were you guys?"

"Well, we had one hell of a problem!" I said.

"You weren't the one with the rope around your neck!"

We both said that we would never do that again, and we didn't. I think that was the most bazaar night I had ever had.

The next morning, still not believing what had happened the night before, I just sat in my room, and pondered what to do. But I could tell what I was going to do now. I am sure all my friends had their suspicions, too.

When we got to work the following Monday, Denny had orders to Hofn, Iceland. We were all sad that he had to go. This remote duty was the worst duty one could get in radar. Damn! The crew was breaking up. We were all thinking back on our good times here. They weren't over yet, but the end was coming soon. Modo got orders to go to Korea. Dave got orders to go to Alaska. And there I was. Reality was hitting me in the face. I wasn't in some school somewhere. I was in the Air Force. The world was becoming a hot potato. The cold war involved us now. It wasn't something we were watching on T.V. It was real.

I think these thoughts I had going through my mind were what convinced me to go to Texas and get married. It was March by that time. I went to Texas with many plans and dreams. When I got there Cathy was excited. We made love, and went to pick up the rings. For some reason, I did not feel at ease about not telling our parents. But I kept my word, and on March 21st we got married at Tarrant County Court House. I thought that I was happy, and I thought she was, too. So we partied with her friends past midnight. I was so drunk, I got sick as hell. I didn't like drinking unless I was high first. I had a headache from hell. I was in the bathroom when Cathy came in. She said I had a phone call from my commanding officer. He told me my leave had been canceled, and I had to report back to base immediately. I complained that I just got married. He told me I was not at my mama's; I was in the Air Force now. I had to report or face charges.

"Yes Sir, Commander Sir. I will have to get a flight."

"I know, airman. You only have 72 hours to get back."

"Yes Sir, Commander Sir. I will notify you of my whereabouts, Sir."

Well, that was that. Cathy asked me what was wrong. I told her I didn't know, but it didn't sound good. She asked me if I had done anything wrong.

I answered, "No, it's not me. But something is up, and it's not good, not good at all. I have to be back within 72 hours."

Cathy asked why I had to go so soon.

"Because when they say jump, I jump. It's the military, girl. I can't get a note from my teacher. This is the way it is when I am in the Air Force."

Cathy was mad. Before I left, she reminded me to make sure I changed my forms to report our marriage. I was surprised by that. Why wouldn't I do that? The little things that most people pick up on were just going right over my head, and it was not apparent to me that I was getting set up by her. I was always taught to be honest and keep my word. The problem was that I could not be honest with myself about my situation, so how could I expect anyone else to be honest. I had my buddies though, and I said my goodbyes to my new wife. My mind was spinning. I was wondering if I would ever see Cathy again. I wondered what was going on that was bad enough that I had to rush back. Things were whirling in my mind, and to be truthful, I don't know what I was thinking.

It took me less than 48 hours to get back, but when I did I found out why they wanted me back. A Mig 23 had flown over Key West and throughout Florida all leave was canceled. The Air Force had a surprise for me, too. I had orders to Thule, Greenland. When I heard that, the first thing that came to mind was my dad. I remembered the day I told my dad I'd joined up. He said that they would send me to Greenland. I figured he had something to do with this. At first I was excited. I knew that it meant space tracking. I also knew they would send me to Colorado Springs for training and that Cathy could come. Then I thought of Denny, Modo, Dave, and J.J. My guys, my friends, my crew. I thought of all the things I would miss; our talks, our parties. Our times together would never again be. It made me sad.

Two days later the Air Force would give me another surprise. I got new orders to Hofn, Iceland; the same place that Denny was going. I called home to tell Mom and Dad, and then I called Cathy to tell her that I had new orders, and that I would be coming home for a little while. I didn't tell her that it was April Fool's Day, and that I only had a 21 day notice. That meant that I had to be in Iceland in 31 days. Denny had to report at the same time. I guess the world wanted us real bad.

The world was a dangerous place at that time. The Cold War with Russia was getting to a level that it had not been since Kennedy was shot. We were at the time of the Hunt for Red October, and Libya. Conflict was breaking out all over the place, with the same shit different day shit that had been going on since Korean War time, and still goes on today. But our government did not want to admit it. The reason was oil! It is all about who can and will control the oil in the world. Like a trained monkey, trying to get a banana; if he could only reach it, he would be satisfied.

Denny and I were packing our bags as Modo and J.J. watched with mixed emotions. We were on our way back to our homes, but this had been our home for awhile, and we did not want to leave. But, we had no choice.

As we said our goodbyes all of us knew that this was the last time we would be with each other. It was an emotional goodbye. I said goodbye to Denny, but we knew we would see each other in Philly. That was our agreement. We would both fly to Philly and go to McGuire Air Force Base. We could at least see some part of the good ole US of A before we went to Iceland together.

As I drove home, I found KAAY again on the radio and somehow felt a little better for a while. That would not last as long as I wanted. As all vacations, they just don't seem to last as long as you would like them to last. I didn't see the storm that was approaching, but it was coming.

CHAPTER 10
The Nightmare Begins

    I got home around two o'clock in the morning. It was a hot night, and I was ready to get in my own bed. My mom and dad were waiting up for me. As I pulled in the driveway, I felt pretty good. I was home, but would it be like before? Would it be like Texas? I didn't know. It was up to God, not me.
    I remember waking up the next day to a bright, sunny day. I was watching the world news on TV. The talk was about Russia, and I could see the worry in my mother's eyes. I asked her if she wanted to go outside and smoke a cigarette with me. We walked outside. I assured her everything would be fine, but she was a mother, and mothers always worry about their sons. I told her I didn't think God's plans were for me to die in that frozen north, but that His plans were greater than Iceland. I told her she would see her son again. I don't think it helped much. I gave her a kiss, and she slowly walked inside the house. My dad didn't show emotions like Mom and I did. We wore our feelings on our sleeves. Dad just kept his inside when he felt pain. He tried to be the tough guy, but he was not fooling me.

The days went by pretty fast and it was now within a week before I was to leave for Philly. I still felt uneasy about not telling our parents that Cathy and I were married, but I was going to keep my word. I was excited and uncomfortable at the same time. It all came down to me keeping my word as I was getting ready to go.

The night before I was to leave, I went over to Cathy's parents' house. I asked them to take care of Cathy for me. I gave her a kiss and told her that I would see her in the morning since she was going with my parents to the airport. I went back to the house. I got home to a quiet, but troubled home. I was off to do my part for our country. The mood was something that I had never felt in my house before.

My dad broke the ice so to speak by asking what I planned on wearing on the plane. I told him I would wear my dress blues. I asked him why he asked. He thought I'd be more comfortable wearing something like jeans. I told him that the jeans there did not fit me anymore, and I just thought that I would wear my blues. That is when my mother got up and went to their bedroom. Dad said just leave her be because she is thinking as a mom does. I told him goodnight. He said goodnight and told me he loved me. I told him I loved him, too. It was like a funeral or something.

I went to bed. My dreams that night were all over the place. In my dreams, I wondered what people all around the world were dreaming about. I was hoping that their dreams were coming true. Suddenly I awoke to a bad strorm outside, and as the lightning violently flashed through my window and the thunder shook the whole house, a limb of the tree by my bedroom broke off and crashed at my window. I was in a cold sweat and confused for a split second when the door to my room opened slowly, and I saw a figure at the door.

It took me a moment to see who it was, then with her voice cracking a little I saw that it was my mother saying, "A.J., it is time."

I said okay and slowly got out of bed and into the shower. The storm still violently raged on as I got dressed for my upcoming flight. I came out of my room as dad was sitting down at the kitchen table. He asked me if I wanted some coffee. I said yes, not because I wanted some coffee, but so I could sit with my mother and father knowing it would be the last time I would do so for awhile. It was a somber moment for us all. My mom started to get teary eyed, and my dad said it was a moment that was special to them. I felt the same.

We went to pick up Cathy at her parents' house and were finally on our way to the airport. Knowing I would see Denny in Philly helped me calm down a little. The scene at the airport was emotional to say the least. I gave my mother and dad a hug, told them I loved them, and then gave Cathy a kiss and hug and told her that everything would be okay.

Her performance could have earned her an Academy Award. I can see that now, but I could not see it then. I truly thought it was real. I got on the plane and watched them on the ground as the plane flew into the sky.

The plane landed in Memphis before going on to Philly. When I got to Philly, I did not know if Denny was there yet, so I walked all around the airport. No Denny. I was getting nervous because he wasn't there. Just when I thought I was going to go crazy, I saw him.

"Hey boy! Where have you been?" I yelled.

He said he got hung up in Chicago so he arrived late. "But I'm here now," he said.

"Damn right you are. How have you been?" I asked.

We walked towards the front of the airport. Philly was a dump. I had always thought about it as the birthplace of liberty. Well, if that's the case then my toilet was freedom. My opinion of Philly would change over time, because I would see towns and scenes that made Philly look like Hawaii.

We went to the information desk and asked about the shuttle that would take us to McGuire AFB. We asked what time it left and how much it would cost to take us there. We found out it was free, and we could wait until the next day to leave. That suited us just fine because we wanted to relax before we went to the base anyway.

We walked to a motel next to the airport and stayed the night. As it turned out it was just what the doctor ordered. It gave us a chance to talk about the times we had in Florida and the reason we were going to Iceland. We knew it was to track Russian planes. Denny was saying that if Iceland was as cold as where he was from we were in for a hell of a time.

I asked him what he wanted to do up there, and his answer surprised me. He wanted to buy a new stereo! Damn! I never thought much about that. I asked him how we would pay for it, and he reminded me of the PX catalog that we could order it from.

We talked about a lot of different things that night. We hoped our stuff was in Iceland when we got there. I told Denny that if we ever got R and R, I'd like to show him Scotland because of my family there. So we talked about Scotland for a bit. I told him it was pretty there, and I told him about the women. I told him if we ever get there he could see for himself. We talked about a lot of other things; people we hoped to see again like our buddies back at Tyndall and friends and family back home.

Then Denny asked me if I told my parents about Cathy. He said, "I know you are a good guy and *your* word is good, but can you trust *her*?"

After thinking, I answered, "I don't know man. I think I should. I guess I'll find out."

Denny said, "I just don't want to see you hurt. I think it will make you bitter, and I love you like a brother, man. I'll whip her ass if she hurts you!"

"Thanks man. That means a lot coming from you. It's more about her now. Shit, I'm going to be in the middle of nowhere. It's not like there's any pussy where we are going."

We talked for a while longer and then went to eat. We got back to the room and watched a little TV and talked some more. I asked him where he would go if he could go anywhere. I told him without hesitation I'd go to Amsterdam! Boy, that would be a place where we could get into a lot of trouble, but we would have one hell of a blast. Damn! I wondered if we would even want to come back from there.

Denny smiled and said, "That would be the million dollar question there, boy!"

As the night wore on, we discussed our mission in Iceland. We wondered what our job would be. The truth was we both really did not know where, or for that matter what we were in for. I decided the best thing we could do is to have each other's back and get home in one piece.

"You got that right! Just make it home."

So we went to sleep not knowing the future that lay in front of us, but we were willing to bet it all. Whatever happened we would be okay.

The next morning we headed back to the airport and caught the shuttle to McGuire. On the way there we met a couple of guys on the airplane who said they too were going to Iceland. One of them had been remote before, and he said we were in for a treat. He said he was glad he was going to get away from his wife and kids for a while. We laughed. We could tell that he had seen many things and been lots of places. He was as interesting to us as all the Vietnam guys were. It was nice to hear their stories and their perspective on things. I don't remember his name, but I will always remember that big smile he had. He said he had seen enough to know that life was too short not to smile when you have made it through war and marriage. He told us he had shit in places that we wouldn't want to shit in much less throw up in before you shit there. He was one hell of a guy.

When we got to McGuire we still had time to walk around a bit, so Denny and I strolled around the flightway for a while. We went back to the overseas terminal and saw the planes that took guys and girls all over the place. It was neat, at least for me. It was like I was a little kid again.

I got to a pay phone and tried to call Cathy, but there was no answer. It was getting about time to go, so one at a time we all went through the line to get on the plane. There were a couple of DC-10s and L10-11s on the ground. I asked Denny if he knew which plane was ours. The sergeant pointed to our ride and said we were not that lucky. The plane he was pointing to was a C-141 transport. Shit! We would get the shitty one. That's when the sergeant smiled and remined us that we were in for a treat.

Denny said, "Oh shit! We are doomed!"

I replied, "Well, I guess that means no stewardesses."

"Yeah, no shit!" Denny said. "My uncle told me about these. The seats face the back of the plane. Damn!"

Sergeant said, "Yes. And when we get there, it's going to be fun watching you wait for your parka because it takes about 36 hours before you get one. And they didn't name that place wrong. It's fucking cold and there you two are in those blues."

"So, the trick's on me Sergeant?"

"Well, you will have to evaluate that yourself, son!"

Oh, fuck! I was thinking to myself. I guess I am in for the treat of my short little life.

We got on the plane and sure enough the seats faced the back of the plane like they were just going to drop us off as they flew by. The pillows were way too small for our heads and the blankets were the military ones. Plus, there were no windows to see out of, so if we were going to crash, we would not know until we crashed.

As the plane was taking off, Denny yelled over the sound of the engines, "I guess we joined the Air Force to aim high!"

I just laughed as we took off. And away we went into the wild blue yonder. People were clapping as the jet roared into the night sky. It was definitely different, but it was not long until I went to sleep; even if we were crammed into the seats like sardines in a can.

About three hours into the flight I had to go to the bathroom, so I got up. It took some doing to even get to the can because of the way we were seated. In the restroom, I was thinking of what Iceland would be like and if was as cold as the sergeant said it would be. I guess I was going to find out soon enough. I wanted to get there to see for myself, and yes, I truly did find out all right.

During the flight Denny turned to me and said, "Well, we are going into a place that we have never been."

"Yeah," I said, "But this is our time to shine; live traffic, brother, live traffic. Not simulations."

"Boy! I never really thought much about it, at least not in that way, but I guess your right."

Denny and I were going into the unknown. He looked back and said again, "I hope our stuff is there."

I think we both were thinking not of our clothes and other necessities, but our pot we both packed in the other stuff.

It didn't take long though for me to think of the reason they sent us to Iceland. We were going to be part of some form of history, and I wondered where that would lead.

About an hour or so later, we landed. We couldn't see the lay of the land. The morning sun was straight up in the sky. It was spitting snow. The wind damn near blew us down when we stepped out of the plane. It was 5:30 in the morning, and everyone had a coat or a jacket except you know who. Shit it was cold. The wind was blowing about 40 to 45 miles per hour, and I could not get warm.

The area had an eerie look to it like I'd seen before in a movie or something like that. It looked like Scotland but without trees. It was a whole lot colder than Scotland, and of course the base was all around us. I am sure we had the "deer in the headlights" look, too. The way we were dressed probably gave away the fact that we'd never been there before.

Our drop off point was the BAQ, and we stayed there until we got our gear. I couldn't wait to get my parka because I was fucking cold! Hell, I was from Arkansas. I thought I knew what cold was. Well, I didn't! I didn't know just how cold it could get!

We hadn't slept much, either. To us, it was about 3:00 in the morning and we were tired. That and the fact that it was 94* when we left McGuire AFB and now it was around 35* made a big difference!

We grabbed a couple hours sleep, and got our parkas, and we were ready to go, but where? Hell, we were in the North Pole! Where could we go?

Then, as we had done many times, we found out where the local hangout was; the NCO Club. We caught a cab and were driven to the club by an Icelandic taxi driver!

The rest of the night we were in kind of a state of bliss. The fun had begun, at least we thought it had. We noticed the local women. How do you tell someone about the women in Iceland? Beautiful! That they were! But, I was married, and it was look, but do not touch for me. Not for Denny, though. Now, that was different. I was talking to the sergeant who was on the plane with us, and I looked around and Denny was gone. I looked outside and didn't see him. I asked the taxi drivers, and nothing. I was getting worried. It was time to be getting back, so the sergeant and I left.

We were on our way to the BAQ when we saw Denny. He looked real fucked up, and when we yelled at him, he grinned that familiar grin, and said, "Sir, do you know where the BAQ is, please?"

I said, "Hell, Denny, it's me! Damn, boy do you know what you are doing?"

"A.J., is that you?"

"Damn, boy, who else knows your name up here?"

You see, drinking beer up here was like drinking three to one at home. It was funny in a way, but it could have cost him his life being out in the elements like that. We got a briefing on that later. That wasn't funny, not funny at all. We got him into the taxi and rode on to the BAQ.

The next morning, we were taken to Recilvic which was about 20 miles away. It was the naval air station in Iceland. Everything was some kind of naval station, even though they were about 80 percent Air Force personel. On the way to the airport, which would take us to

Hofn, we noticed for the first time the beauty of this part of the country. It was green with buildings of all different colors and shapes. There were mountains in the background. It was beautiful.

We were going to the radar station in Rockville, the capital. It was not such a remote place. As far as the rest of the world's standard, it was a small town. But, this was not the rest of the world. This was Iceland, and there was not a big city of any kind within a thousand miles. At least, it didn't seem that way. This was truly the middle of nowhere.

We boarded a small plane called a Focker. It only seated a few people. That seemed appropriate because the flight was to nowhere. We just didn't know that yet. I, myself, never liked small prop planes. They were dangerous. When we took off, we didn't know we were going to a place that could be dangerous depending what one chose to do. We found that out when we arrived.

We were in the middle of nowhere. We saw why they named it Iceland. Ice was all we could see; yes, ice. A hundred miles in either direction was the biggest glacier I have seen to this day. A cold chill slithered down my spine. Was that a clue of the approaching future?

Not long after that the captain said something in Icelandic with a Norwegein flavor, "We are starting our decent. Please buckle your seat belts and place your seats and tray tables in the upright position." It would be a while before we would hear that again.

Most everyone was looking outside and we saw the water. That was all we could see as we decended. It seemed like we would land in the water. I wondered where the runway was. I guessed everyone who had landed there for the first time wondered the same. I was a little worried that we were truly going to drop into the sea. It was most unnerving. Then we landed on, of all things, a gravel runway.

We slowly came to a stop right in front of a Ward's Manufacturing bus that was built in my home town of Conway, Arkansas! That was quite unnerving, too. I hoped it was not one of the buses built when I worked there, because when I worked there, I was tripping most of the time. I remembered the time they tried to start one of the buses, and instead of starting, the horn beeped. I began to see the irony of it all. Shit! I looked up toward the sky and said, "God, I get it. It is you playing a trick on me!" I looked out, not at a terminal as one does at any other airport, but at a one room shack.

"Damn!" Denny said.

Damn is right, I thought to myself. The eerie site I saw was not only the true size of the glacier we had flown over, but the place where we had landed. It was like we had landed on the moon; I saw no trees, no houses, only a mountain that was mostly volcanic rock and ice, and a handful of people. As we loaded into a bus, I couldn't believe how anybody could live here. That was all I could think about. How in the world could anyone live here?

The airman drove us, and it became apparent that we were here for one reason, and one reason only; to do a job. I didn't look forward to that huge mountain beside us being our view for awhile. I saw two big towers, and eight or nine concrete buildings, and a big, white dome. Later we crossed the road and saw Bat Mountain and the black beach below it. As I looked down there, I saw some guys. Then a wave crashed against the rock behind them, and the water rose to about 50 feet in the air. It was a quite a sight to see.

All the guys yelled, "Hey, newbies, welcome to Hofn, boys!"

It was like a scene out of a horror movie.

Denny said, "I think we are in hell!"

"Maybe we are," I answered. "So, let's make the best of it."

We went to the commander's office to meet him, and he seemed to be a pretty good guy. The first sergeant was a vet who had his shit together. Then we went on to the airmen's barracks. This would be our home for awhile.

The guys there were pretty cool. They asked us questions about home. Then we were led to our rooms and we met our roommates. That was a relief, because we could not have picked better ones. Then we got the best news of all. Our stuff was in! We got our stuff, unpacked, and the party started.

My roommate was from South Africa. He was crazy and very different. And there was Donny from Texas, and his long time friend Jose. Both were great guys, and in time became good friends of mine. Then there was Dixie, Lonny, and Doc. Doc was one of a kind. So, here we all were in this surreal place to do a job and work together and get along for at least 12 months.

We went up to operations to take a look at where we would be working. To my my surprise most of the work was to be done by the same guys that were in our barracks. It was like my parents' nursing home business. The backbone of what was done there was done by the nurses. They did the real work as we were going to do. But as in all businesses, directions have to come from the officers, and we had the best, with a couple of exceptions.

On the way back from operations, we found out who was cool, and who was not. We got the cool guys together in our room, and showed them our gifts. I felt like Santa Claus. You would have thought that these guys had never been high. One guy said it had been so long that he had thought of giving it up altogether.

For Denny and me, we could not have had a better first day. That is, until I stepped outside. Shit! The wind picked me up and blew me up against the a building. A couple of the guys told me I'd better know what the weather is before going outside or I'd end up in Bat's Cave. I asked them what that was. They showed us a place that looked like God had taken an ice pick or those sharp tongs that pick up huge ice blocks and lifted a big chunk out of the cliff all the way down to the ocean. Every couple of seconds the water would rush in and blow up in the air about 50 feet, then go back down.

Lonny said, "If I was you, I would try to get along with everyone here 'cause if you are not careful, you will end up in there. If that happens, there's no coming back."

Then my roommate said, "Yeah, and don't go in the ocean."

One of the captains getting high in my room said, "If you fall in, you might last fifteen minutes. That's how cold the water is."

Shit! What a fucking surreal place we were in. We ain't in Kansas anymore, Toto. I went back to get Denny. I just had to show him. Everyone in my room came back outside with us. A wave crashed up against the rocks which were a little over 50 feet high and blew up over a light tower that was next to the site.

Denny said. "Damn, we are in hell!

One of the other guys said, "I bet you never thought hell would be this cold."

CHAPTER 11
Hofn...Did I Make A Mistake?

In Iceland, we were going to be waiting, watching, and listening to everything the Russians were doing. I do not think that the American people, or for that matter, the Russian people knew just how close we were to World War III in that summer of 1978. I know I did not know until I arrived here.
The first week in Hofn, started off with a bang. We didn't know how much traffic we would have there until we started the first day of work. My first shift mayday exercises started with incoming bears, badgers, and backfires. Those were the different Russian bombers. The bears were the long range bombers and the badgers and backfires were the mid-range ones. The backfires and badgers would pactice coming in at us just close enough for us to see them on our scopes. Then they'd back out. They were practicing runs that they'd make in time of war. That would be the way they would take us out with a chemical bomb of some type. We had about 6 or 8 hundred of them a year to keep an eye on.
It was cool to be in that job at that time, and during all the excitement going on that week, I didn't even have time to worry about

not having a telephone to talk to anyone back home. We did not have TV, telephone, or radio, and for that matter we didn't have a real road to go anywhere to a telephone either.

We did a lot of simple things to pass the time. We went for walks, we'd try to climb the 4000 foot mountain that was next to us, or we'd go down to the beach. It was nothing like being in the USA where just about anything was available. We'd get drunk, or get high and play cards. Every once in a while we would get a movie. I was able to listen to more music.

After a while, Denny and I, and almost everyone who was there took advantage of the little store we had. We ordered our stereo and bought a few new albums that we did not have already. That was cool, very cool. There were times when we would pull our speakers out into the hallway and jam. Hell, what else could we do!

All this time, everyone was getting mail but me. I guess it was two weeks before it started to set in that maybe getting married was a mistake. It was really getting to me, and it was starting to show. At least that was what Denny was saying.

"A.J.," he said, "Man, you got to tell someone what is bugging you. And if you don't, I will!"

I just kept walking to the mailroom every day knowing nothing would be there. But, I still had hope that Denny and I were wrong.

I became friends with one of the guys named Jelly. He was a stir crazy black guy from San Antonio, Texas. He and I came up with a way to mail pot to ourselves. We'd put the pot into a couple of baggies, put two coats of wax around it, then put it into a big peanut butter jar and mail it to ourselves. It worked pretty well, so it became a good way for us to be able to stand the place and make money at the same time.

The job became harder as winter came. I still did not get any mail, and I had to listen to my dad bitch me out about money every time he wrote. He wondered what I was doing with my money.

I was working out and getting high just so I could bear this place. I think all of us had something going on that made it worse to be here. Bigfoot was a great guy who did not get high, but was still one of us. This man could bench press a whole universal without breaking a sweat, and then he'd out play us at basketball. He was a great guy. We played with the local team. Well, everything in Iceland was local, but that did not mean that we were all close. We'd always beat our opponent thanks to Bigfoot.

When we went to the main base it was in groups of five or seven because that's just how it worked. One day, I went down with Jelly and Bigfoot and a couple of other guys because I had to see the dentist. The doc said I had a cavity. It turned out that the dentist gave me a shot, pulled all my wisdom teeth, and sent me on my way. About an hour after that, I stormed back to the dentist in a lot of pain, and said, "I don't think so, Bud!" That time I left with something for the pain.

Bigfoot had not been anywhere in seven months, and we were afraid that he might go off on someone. When I got back from the dentist office, we were both on edge. We were ready for a drink. We all got into a taxi and went to the club. We were not in the mood to be fucked with and we needed a drink bad. At the club there was an unwritten rule that a certain table was for the marines. Well, we were remote, unaware of this rule, so we ended up at that table.

While we were sitting there having a drink a cocky, little jarhead came up to us and said, "You stupid sons of bitches! Don't you know this table is reserved for marines?" And then he slapped Bigfoot right across the face.

The look on Bigfoot's face was indescribable! Jelly and I jumped up. Then Bigfoot got up. The stupid jarheads about shit their pants.

The little guy said, "Oh, shit! Are we in trouble now!"

That's when Bigfoot hit him so hard that he went flying over the bar into the mirror, breaking it into pieces. I did a spinning back fist, and Jelly kicked the other one in the nuts.

The whole bar stood up and cheered, and Bigfoot stood over them and said, "Who is stupid now, boys?"

After that, we heard that they put a sign on that table saying "This table is for Hofn only". We had a lot of fun with that.

It was winter by this time, and it was not a good time for many of us. I told the guys what was going on with me. I kept hoping that I would get a letter or something in the mail. While everyone else ran to see if they had gotten some mail, I just walked slowly because I knew I'd get zero every day.

Being winter, the wind was blowing about 50 to 85 knots, and it was snowing all the time. We would see an officer in his cunt cap and pop one on him and his cap would go flying. One captain came around the building one time and the wind picked him up and slammed him face down into the sidewalk. We did not see him again.

There was Gary, too. He was a young guy from Hastings, Nebraska. He had been there for three months when he found out his mother died. He had helped his mother raise his six younger brothers after his dad ran off. Of course, the military would not let him go home. I still to this day do not understand that way of thinking. He had trouble with that. Hell, anybody would.

I was playing cards one night and Doc said to me, "We do not need another Bigfoot problem, so I think you need to talk to someone about your situation, A.J. You are too wound up to go off this way. I have told the boss about it."

"Why, man?"

"Shit! With what you know! Hell! We're all too scared to say anything. Man, you could kill somebody and you know it."

He was right. I was in a killing state. Being winter didn't help. The only thing I had going for me was that I had the guys and the northern lights to look at. The lights were a sight to behold. It was just one of those things that showed you that there was a God. In their splendor, they were the best fireworks show I have ever seen.

I knew I had to do something to get to Cathy. It was eating away at me. I really did not know what I would do, but I had to get out of there or I was going to hurt somebody. And I still walked to the mail room alone and in pain that I had never felt before. How could someone you love do this? And why?!! My answer never came, and I walked to the mailroom again and again.

It was Christmas by now, and I stayed while a lot of guys went home. We worked straight shifts for a couple of days. They kept telling us that a big blizzard was coming, but we kept waiting. We got a few hours off, and we were in our little club when one of the new guys walked in with snow all over him.

Doc said, "Let's go outside and play football!"

"Hell, yes!" we said. There we were, the wind blowing us all around. It was snowing so hard we could not even see the ball, much less each other. We had a blast!

The next morning we could not get out of our barracks. My roommate opened up the window and put his beer out in the snow drift. I asked him what he was doing. He said it was better than the fridge. I just laughed. A couple days later it was so bad that we could not even get any food up there. If any of us got hurt or something went wrong, we were fucked because we would die.

A couple more days went by, and the only thing we had for breakfast, lunch, and dinner was tuna. And, it was not the tuna like we got at home. After that experience, it took a long time before I would eat tuna again.

By the time all the guys were back from the holidays, I told my sergeant, "If you don't find a way to get me out of here, I'm going to fuck something or someone up! You get me?" He knew from what Doc had told him that I was not joking.

AWAC was on the island, and boy did those guys have fun when they first got up there. Being a skilled tech had its advantages for me. I got to the main base and hopped on with an AWAC crew going to Oklahoma City, and away I went.

It was New Year's Day and we were high over northern Canada. We were listening to the Rose Bowl on the radio. It was great to hear a radio after such a long time, but my mind was on someone else. It took six hours to get to the base. I think it could have been longer, but it didn't take me long to get from Tinker AFB to the airport.

I tried to call Cathy then, but got no answer. It took only 45 minutes to get to Dallas. Cathy was going to modeling school in Arlington. I knew that something was up when I called again three more times, and there still was no answer. I thought maybe maybe she had gone home for the holidays. My mind was all over the place. It was apparent that I made another mistake by going there, but I had to know something or I was going to blow.

It was about two more hours before the pay phone I had been using rang, and I answered it.

"Is someone calling me from this number?" Cathy asked.

I said, "Yea, there is. The guy you married."

"A.J.!" she yelled.

"Well, who else have you married lately?"

She asked where I was. When I told her I was at DFW, she told me she'd be right there to pick me up. In about 20 or 30 minutes she arrived with some girlfriend of hers and some guy. I knew in my mind that he was the one. But it didn't hit me then. That came later, a lot later.

All I could think of was her. I did not say anything until we were alone. She looked like shit. I could tell she was on something, and it was not just pot. It was crystal meth, and I knew it.

I didn't plan what to say exactly, but I was just sitting there and it popped out. "I was in the middle of the Arctic Circle. Why have you not written me in what, eight months? Have you been too busy?"

"No," she answered. I left it at that. And when she wanted to make love, well let's just say if you were a man that had not had any since the last time you had been with this woman, what would you say? That was a no brainer.

I was so tired that I fell asleep after. But, after being in Iceland doing what I do for living, I had become a light sleeper. I awoke when I heard her talking low to someone on the phone. I was not openminded to the fact that there was someone else in her life. It was the worst four days of my life.

When I got back to the Hofn, Denny told me that they had been talking about me and Jose asked him, "Denny, you know him better than anyone. What do you think?"

Denny answered, "When a guy can kill with one punch, it is best to leave that guy alone."

Denny told the sergeant that they all thought I needed to go on R and R as soon as possible. About a month later, Denny told me that we were headed to Amsterdam! I was ready. It only took about a couple of hours to get there from the main base. I wondered what it would be like there. I really didn't know. I had never been to that part of Europe.

It was more than I expected. It was crazy, and it was just what the doctor ordered. Amsterdam was a pretty place with all kinds of beautiful houses, canals, and shops. It had everything that I was looking for on my break from the stress. Not knowing that I was an addict at that time, I couldn't see the real effects of my choices. Just about everyone around me knew, though. That was the rub.

We went to the hotel. It was cool, but the coffee shop is what blew my mind. We saw something we'd never see in the states. It was cool, and then some. We walked in and the counter was nothing but pot. I mean pot from all over the world. We drooled. If you got soup, it had a pot leaf in it. If you went to the smoking room, it was full of pot. Hell, we got stuck in there. I don't think I have ever been that high on pot before. When we walked out, a guy asked if we were Americans and if we liked hash.

"Hell, yes," we answered.

He said, "Ten dollars."

We thought he meant per gram, but he handed us a handful!

We asked where the hookers were, and some guy pointed to the beautiful women in the windows. I thought I must have been in heaven. Ten on a ten scale; they were beautiful. They gave us some head that would start a leaf blower. I will never forget those three days in Amsterdam.

When we got back to the site, I had a good feeling about myself and how to deal with my situation. I found out that Denny and Jose and Gary had new orders and were going to be leaving soon. That bumped me out because Denny and I had been together for over two years now. It was a terrible feeling. Lonny was gone, and so was Jelly, Dixie, and Bigfoot. It was hard for me to say goodbye. These guys had helped me through a difficult time, and they were leaving.

We decided to throw a toga party. We took pictures. It was a blast. Everyone dressed in togas of some sort. I wore my Razorback longjohns and put a sheet around me. I am sure we all looked like fools, and we all got very drunk. After being cooped up in the North Pole for a year, we had to let off some steam somehow.

It was the end of an era for us. We made it through a time in history. It would not be in the history books, but we knew we were as close to WW III as anytime in our history. American people didn't have a clue, either.

I was sad that my friends were gone, and I hoped to see them again. But, with the military, who knows. Gary, the kid from Hastings, was sent to Bergstrom AFB in Austin, Texas, and then I got orders to go there, too. I was told later that Gary told everyone there that one crazy mother-fucker was coming to Bergstrom and his name was A.J.

The last few days in Iceland were tough, but what I missed the most was my friends that I knew I'd probably never see again, and that sucked. My time in Iceland was, at the same time, the best of times and the worst of times for me. I took a lot of memories with me, and I will cherish them forever.

When I left Iceland, I found out that I only had four days to report to the base. I didn't even have a car. I wanted to see my parents to tell them the truth. I guess I knew what I needed to do, but I was not looking forward to it. I knew my path was set, and I was not going to go down the same one again in the near future. It was what I had to do.

CHAPTER 12
Back to the Real World....The Last and A First

    I think God does for us what we can't do for ourselves, and through the pain we can find what we need.
    Well, I was back in the US of A, and it was like I had never left. I knew that the world might not have changed, but I had. It was good to be home though, and I also knew that there was something I had to do before I reported to my next duty station. I needed to tell the truth and stand up for myself. Of course, I wanted my belongings because by now I had quite an album collection; almost one thousand albums, and counting. I wanted my stereo and other things I had gathered along the way.
    I got on the plane to St. Louis. I had mixed emotions. I had to call my parents first. I had not heard from Cathy. I was still hoping that she would be at the airport, but I knew in my mind that she would not. I guess I was in some way holding on to a sliver of hope. I didn't know why. I called home when I got to St. Louis, and my mother answered the phone.
    "Hello, Mom. I told you I'd be okay."

"Oh, Honey, it's A.J.," Mom shouted to my dad. "Where are you?"

"I am in St. Louis. I'll be coming to Little Rock at about 7:00pm."

Mom told me they would be there to pick me up. She also said she loved me. I got on the plane for the short flight to Little Rock. When I landed, it seemed funny in a way. I didn't feel like I had been gone. It was strange, but the minute I saw my parents, I knew what it meant for them to see me. I hugged them both and told Dad that I only had three days before I had to be in Austin.

He was talking about getting up the next morning and taking me to Wynne, Arkansas to get a car from my brother-in-law's dad. That's when I asked them if they had heard from Cathy. They just looked at me with this blank stare. They told me they hadn't seen her in months. I told them I had hoped that she'd come to the airport. I could see that they knew I was hurt, but they had no idea. I am sure they did not know what was coming. On the drive home, I told them I wanted to go to her parents' house and see what they had heard. What I really wanted to do is see what Mel, her sister, knew because I knew she would know something.

It was nice to sleep in my old bed again, and I knew then that I was home, finally home. I slept like a baby, and the next morning I went over to Cathy's parents' house. I drove into the driveway, got out, and walked up and rang the doorbell. When the door opened it was Mel. She threw her arms around me and started crying.

"Where is she, Mel?"

"I don't know, A.J."

I knew she was holding back, but at the same time I believed her because I truly do not think she knew. But she knew something.

Mel asked me, "What are you going to do?"

I answered, "Well, I have to go to Wynne and get a car, so I will be back later."

She told me she was glad I was back, and I left.

It wasn't long before Dad and I left to go to Wynne. On the way, we were talking and he turned to me and started in on me just like always.

"What did you do with the money you made? And don't tell me you spent it up there."

I said, "I'll tell you what!" And here it came. "On March 21st, 1978 at Tarrant County Court House, Cathy and I were married, and she has been getting half of my money, and I haven't even got a letter from her since I got there!"

You would have thought I had hit him over the head with a shovel. He started crying, "Why? Why didn't you tell me the truth?"

"Because I gave her my word! I made a mistake, Pop!"

"Do her parents know?" he asked.

"No!"

"Well, they are going to know now."

Before we got back to Conway, I called my mother and told her to have Cathy's parents meet us at the house. She didn't know what was going on, but she did it.

The drive home was quiet. There wasn't another word said. I think my dad was stunned. When we got to the house, Cathy's parents were there. I walked in with my dad. They were all sitting, and I blurted it out. It was quite a scene. Her dad tried to call her over and over. After about five tries, she answered. He went off on her. He told her that we were all coming to Arlington to get her.

It was about midnight when we left. I slept the entire six hour drive. We stopped at a pancake house just outside of Arlington, and her dad called her. He came to our table and said Cathy was on her way to the restaurant.

I saw her get out of a red car so I walked to the front door of the restaurant to meet her. She looked like shit. When I opened the door and said hello to her she bumped into me and said, "I'm sorry, sir." She kept walking into the restaurant. She didn't even know me! My heart broke. It was the last straw.

When she got to the table, our parents must have told her that was me at the door, and she ran outside and threw her arms around me. She told me she was sorry and that she was tired. Yeah, right. I thought. I was the one that was fucked over, not her.

We went to a motel because our parents needed some rest before they drove us back home. We got our own room and made love, but there wasn't any feeling. It was just cold, very cold.

When we got back to Conway we did not have time to do anything but say goodbye. We left for Texas. My dad gave me directions to some family friends in Austin, and away we went. About half the way there she said that her dad had given her enough money to rent a Uhaul to get her stuff in Arlington. She said her friends would help her load it, and they would drive it to Austin for us.

We arrived in Arlington, loaded all her things, and went on our way to Austin. What was funny was that about halfway to Austin, she wanted to ride with her friend instead of me. I guess she thought I was clueless to what was really going down.

When we got to Austin, my parents' friends, Gary and Jen, were waiting on us and they showed us our new place. We unloaded about half of the things in the UHaul, and I had to get some sleep. Cathy's friend slept on the couch, and Cathy and I slept together.

In the morning I had to report to base, and I knew I would be only a little while. Cathy and her friend thought I'd be all day, I'm sure. When I got back to the apartment and opened the door, I caught them in bed together. She just sat there half clothed. He walked by me as if he was in charge of the situation. But, he didn't know me. And it was pretty obvious that she didn't know me either.

I laid down the rules. "I want the bumb out of here, and if you stay then you will say goodbye to this piece of shit. Or, go with him and get out of my life forever!"

She ran to him. It did not take long for her to make up her mind.

It was too late for me to care. After Cathy left, Gary brought Jen and Wayne to my apartment. They didn't know what was going on, but it wasn't too hard to figure it out.

Jen looked and me and said, "I'm sorry for your pain."

I looked into her eyes and felt something that I had never, and I mean never, felt before. It was love at first sight. I think it was for her, too. But, I didn't want to get in between her and her boyfriend. I didn't want to do what my so called wife had done to me. Out of respect, I kept my feelings to myself, and she did too.

It wasn't long before Cathy and her boyfriend took the car and left. I did not see her again for a while, and it was during this time that she, being high on speed one night, called her parents and said that I had run off and she did not know where I was. Our parents flew down to Austin and they got to my apartment and rang the doorbell. They were shocked when I answered the door.

"Where have you been?" they asked.

"I'm in the Air Force. Where do you think I've been?" I said.

They told me what Cathy had told them. Then I explained to them what was going on. I guess they were shocked. Before they left, I told my dad to file for divorce for me, and he said he would. That would be the last time our parents were good friends because of what Cathy was doing to me and what she was doing to herself.

Parents almost always take their children's word to be truthful. The truth is usually overshadowed by their love for their child. They do not want to see things as they truly are. That's how it usually works until it becomes obvious that the truth has been clouded.

CHAPTER 13
Alone in Austin

    It was around this time that I became friends with a couple of guys that were involved with the Mexican cartel. I was also friends with Gary and Ford. Ford was Jen's boyfriend, but I didn't like the way he treated her. Part of that probably was because of my feelings for her. I was confused not knowing if I was just having a rebound effect, or if my feelings for Jen were real. Either way, I knew I felt something. We became friends long before anything else happened. Mainly because I didn't want to make the same bad decisions that I had made before. I was very cautious at this time.
    The guys at the squadron were cool, and we hung together, too. I was trying to adjust to being stateside. Meth had become the big thing at the time, and I started making runs for the cartel. It was risky, but I made twice as much in two trips as I did in a whole month in the service.
    Jen and I became closer and closer, and Ford did not like that much. There was nothing going on, though. We also became friends with a couple of guys that had just gotten out of the Air Force. Living

in Austin was great, not only because of the atmosphere, but because of all the new friends I was meeting. Things were changing for me.

Austin was a great place for music. There was Willie's Picnic and the Armadillo World Headquarters. The cops were not allowed inside there. I remember many times going to the Armadillo and pitching coins into a hat. Stevie Ray Vaughn would be playing and smoking a joint. We'd blow the smoke at the cops outside. I also got to see Van Halen, the Who, and Bad Company while I was in Austin.

This was also a time when Iran took the hostages at the Embassy, and things were getting a little ditsy. I went TDY (tour of duty assignment) a lot. I went to a lot of places like Washington State and California. I was making more money than I had ever made. Violence was involved, too. I remember one run especially. When we got back, the cartel blew the driver's head off right in front of me. I just knew they were going to kill me, but they just said, "Hey! I say! Did you see anything?"

I said, "No, man! I did not!"

I do not know why, but I only knew that it was not me lying there with half a head left. I couldn't understand anything anymore. Where were my feelings? All I did know was how I felt for Jen. The rest was all over the place. My commitment to the Air Force and what I was into off base were running together. I did not like where it was taking me.

I got a new apartment and it was closer to the base and Jen's place. Our love was growing. By this time, Ford had left, and Jen and I were hanging out together. Even she didn't know what I was into on the outside, though.

My car was in Cathy's hands, and I needed a new one. My parents got me a new Toyota Corona. Before I got it, though, I asked Gary to borrow his car so I could take Jen on a date. Jen and I were to the point that we knew we were best friends, and both of us wanted more. I took her out on a date and we both had a great time. After that, we were joined at the hip. She went everywhere I went, except when I was doing "the other thing". I didn't want that life for her, and I was trying to get out of it, too, but it wasn't that easy.

The world politics helped me in that endeavor by sending me all over the place TDY. But, I still had my connections. We were doing a lot of drugs. You name it, we did it, and life seemed to be good.

Then it came; the first time we made love. Boy, when you find your soul mate in life, it is a wondrous thing. I don't think I will ever forget that night or the next morning. Ever! I did not know at this time that Jen was going to have a baby. I think that Ford had gotten her pregnant and just got mad that she loved me and not him. So, he said fuck it and got out of the Air Force. He said the baby wasn't his, but he wasn't man enough to do what was right, so he left. She didn't know what to do.

It was Thanksgiving time, and my parents, along with my sister and her husband, were down to give me the car and to spend the holiday with me.

I had to go in to the base Thanksgiving morning only to come back to my apartment to find a U-haul in front of my place, and to find Cathy and her parents there trying to take everything I had. They tried to start some shit about Jen, too. I amost got into it with her, but I just let them take the stuff and leave. It was quite a scene.

That was also the day when Jen told me that she was going to have a baby, and the Air Force was going to kick her out. That's just what they did to girls back then.

So I sat her down, and we talked about things. I did not want to be wrong twice. I told her if she was going to have this baby, she was not going to do anymore drugs! And if she loved me, she would have to be honest with me about the way she felt about us. I wanted to know if she was going to stay here or go home. I wanted her to prove to me that she wanted me not because she had to, or because she had nowhere else to go, but because she wanted to be with me!

She did just that! We were always together, and for the first time in my life I felt loved. It was a special time for both of us. It was the little things that were key for me. The way she acted, the way she had her way of... well anybody who's been in love would know what I was saying.

I remember when she was getting bigger and bigger. One time we were kissing and she started laughing. I asked her what was so funny. She said it was the first time her stomach touched a person before her tits did. I guess you just had to be there to understand. That was how we were. I will always know that she was my soul mate. She was and still is the most beautiful woman, both phsyically and mentally, I have ever known. We were in love and talked about everything.

My parents knew how we felt about each other, and they didn't say anything bad at all, which was unusal. Our love grew along with her waist. It was a wonderful time in my life. Jen had a glow about her that made her even more beautiful to me at that time.

We needed money so I got back into the "game" for a short period of time. That was a tough time for us both. One time someone broke into Ray's house. He was one of my connections. Jen and Gary went with me to Ray's house. He thought I was the one who broke into his house. Well, we got over to his house and the guy pulled a gun on me! Jen and Gary were standing there. He put the gun right to my eyes and said, "I'm going to kill you right in front of your friends. What do you think about that, white boy?"

I said, "Pull the trigger. Then the next time someone steals from you, you can kill the next guy. Will that make you the big man then?"

He put the gun down, and Jen and Gary took a deep breath. Then Jen hit Gary in the face and said, "Why didn't you do something?"

He answered, "What! Like get shot along with him?"

Ray thought about it for a while and said he was sorry! He was just pissed off.

I said, "It's OK, but the next time you better pull the trigger because I'm going to kill you if you ever do that again. Do you understand, Boy? I'll kill you dead. OK?"

I never had another problem out of him again.

February came, and I was going to California again. By this time there was a tech sergeant that was in charge of our squad at the squadron. He was a shit. You know the type. 35-10 all the way. The major that was our officer in charge told this guy that he would have to prove himself to us because we had overseas experience, and we didn't like guys from the wing who just thought they could come in here and make us jump when he said jump. The major told him to be careful because he would lose any respect we had for him if we didn't beat the hell out of him. Well, he didn't go along with that way of thinking. This guy was one of those who thought he hung the moon. Well, he was warned, and so someone made sure he didn't make that mistake again.

March came along, and I went to California again. Jen was having a tough time doing anything, and I knew it. But she wouldn't say anything about how she was feeling. I did not want to leave her, but I had no choice being in the Air Force, so I had some friends watch out for her while I was gone. I also had to go with Jose to south Texas to get some "stuff", if you know what I mean. Jen thought that I was still in California, but I was on my way back to Austin by way of south Texas, not by U.S. transport. She also did not know that I had to turn around three days later and go to Ft. Bragg, North Carolina. I think the history books will tell why we were there in late March of 1980. We were into so many things at that time it was hard to keep up.

As Jose and I were driving back from south Texas, our forward lookouts heard on the CB radio that the border patrol were looking for a small car, silver in color, with Arkansas plates. They thought it was carrying drugs to Austin. We had to dump the stuff. We got stopped, and had to go through interrogations. It didn't make things any better for me that our guys found out that it was someone in Austin that ratted us out. We were clean, and they had to let us go.

We had our contacts lead the guys that we thought were the rats to my apartment so we could take them on a last ride. We just didn't figure that Jen would walk in on us pointing all kinds of guns at theses guys. When she did walk in on us, it scared her half to death. I didn't want her to be any part of that part of my life, and in that regard I felt terrible about it. She slapped me around and cursed me for about two hours. I promised her that it was the last time I would ever be in that position, or put her or the baby in that position again. I kept that promise.

It was March 24th I believe, and I never dreamed of what would happen next. Jen was about seven months into the pregnancy. I was at the base that day. She went down to do the laundry and fell down the stairs. She didn't tell me because she didn't want to worry me and she didn't think it was a bad fall. She felt okay later, too.

When I got back from base, she asked me where I was going. She had a feeling that I was going to be gone, but she didn't know how long I'd be gone. We talked for a couple of hours.

"My life has become so fucked up, Jen, I don't know what I'm doing anymore."

"I knew you were into something. Whatever it is, it has changed you into someone else. I want back the man I fell in love with."

"That guy is still here. I am going to fight and get back that person you can have faith in again."

I wanted to get myself back as well. We kissed and held each other tight as we both fell asleep in each others arms. I prayed for the first time in a long time before I fell asleep. I didn't know that God had already decided to do for us what we couldn't do for ourselves. I also didn't know it would be in such a way that it turned out to be.

Jen cried out in pain, and I jumped in shock. The scream frightened me!

"What's wrong, Baby?" I said. "What's happening?"

She answered, "I don't know, but it's not good."

With little notice she was going into labor, and I surely didn't know what the hell to do. I did know I needed to get her to the hospital as soon as I could. I think it was truly the first time I thought I was going to lose her. I must have driven 100 miles an hour getting to the hospital. When we got there she was in extreme pain.

As I banged on the door I screamed, "We need help!!! Help!!! She is having a baby!! Help us please!"

A guy in the stairwell told the nurses he could hear someone yelling for help downstairs. They opened the door, and got Jen to the doctors. I was right beside her all the way. I prayed the entire way up. They took her to surgery immediately. They were going to take the baby.

Twenty-five minutes later, a nurse rushed out of the operating room carrying something in her arms. I was more afraid than I had ever been. The doctor came out and told us that Jen was okay, but the baby had some bad problems. She was deaf and dumb, paralyzed, and wouldn't live through the night. I was in total shock. I didn't know what I would tell Jen. How could someone tell her that her baby was not going to survive. I just didn't know how to tell her.

The doctor asked me if I wanted to see my baby. I went to ICU and the nurses took me to see Didi. That was the name Jen had picked, and we both loved that name. I really did not know how I was going to react. I was already crying as the nurses led me to where Didi was. I felt a sense of fear.

When I saw her she looked so small and frail. I was afraid to get close to her. They told me to wash my hands and use the gloves that were part of her incubator that she lay in. I held her in my arms and I felt God's presence. We looked into each others eyes, and I don't care what anybody says about newborns not knowing what they are looking at. I knew she could see me, and that God was telling me that this girl was going to be just fine. I knew it to be true.

Our friends were in the room with Jen by this time, and when I walked in they started to cry. They asked me about the baby because the nurse had already told them that Didi wasn't going to make it. I said to them that our baby was going to be just fine. Yes, she had some very bad problems, but I had just seen her and I don't know why, but I knew that baby was going to make it.

When the nurse came back I asked her to get her supervisor. Just as she walked out the doctor came in and said that they were going to have to operate on Didi because she had an open spine defect and needed surgery as soon as possible. The nurse supervisor came in and asked us not to tell Jen when she awoke. They wanted me to be the one to tell her later.

By this time it was about 6:30 a.m., and I had to go to the base to tell my major what had happened. I needed to report that I needed to be at the hospital. My friends stayed with Jen while I went to the base. When I got there they were not very happy with me. They said it wasn't my problem, and if I left they would slap an Article 15 on me when I got back from my mission. The major asked me if I loved Jen.

I said, "I love them both; her and the baby. If you really want me to pick, then you might as well put those handcuffs on me now, Sir!"

"No, sir, I won't give you a 15 because you are too important to us, and I hate to do the wrong thing for the wrong reasons. You just get back here in time to go TDY, or I will!"

"Yes, sir, Major, sir." It was nice to have an officer who knew how to be an officer and stand up for his men.

I knew that God was doing for us what we could not do for ourselves, and that at least for the time, I was a father and my life had changed for the best. That was an eye opening moment in my life that would carry me through because I had a family of my own now, and the bad choices of the past would have to stay in the past. They had no place in my life anymore, at least for now. I had been touched by a little child that was from God.

So I went back to see how my girls were doing, and when I got there Didi had gone through surgery with flying colors. Then, I got bitched out by Jen.

"How's my daughter, and why did they have to operate?"

That made me mad because I had given orders to the nurses to let me tell Jen about Didi. They didn't do their job, and Jen was crying. It took all I could do to calm her down.

"Baby, she is not doing so well, but I saw her last night and I truly believe that she is going to be okay."

"How do you know?"

I answered, "Baby, I just know. I don't know how, but I believe that and you must believe it too if we are going to get through this together! I love you. Do you believe that?"

"Yes, I do!" she answered.

"Baby, you know I have to go for awhile," I reminded her.

"Yes, I remember, Baby."

"I have Pam and Bill and all our friends ready to keep a check on you while I'm gone." I told her they were all ready to help.

When a person is in the military, personal feelings cannot be put in front of what has to be done for the military. It just doesn't work that way. I didn't need an Article 15 to be on my record. At the same time though, I could not keep my feelings for my future wife and my daughter out of my mind. The fact was they were all that was on my mind.

When I got on the plane with the other guys, we couldn't believe that we were flying on regular airlines. We knew this mission had to be something that we'd never been involved with before. No, sir, this was not the normal misson at all. Still, my mind was on Jen and Didi. They were the new focus in my life now.

When we arrived at Fort Bragg, we found out what our job was. We were to try to find a way to bring the hostages home from Iran. My mind started racing. I needed to get word to my parents that I wasn't in Austin. I needed to find out how Jen and Didi were. That was the main thing on my mind; not the job at hand. My mind should have been on my mission.

It took a couple of days, but I found a way to get off the base and call my parents. When I called them, I really wanted to say many things to them, but I knew I had to be quick. So I just told them I loved them, and that I might be in Iran the next day. I asked them to take care of Jen and the baby. That was all I said.

I went back to the base and we took off on our mission. We got to Iran, and the rest is history. We felt a sense of failure after the mission. In my opinion, our country hasn't learned one fucking thing about who or what we are fighting and why. We have only to look in the mirror to find the answer to our problems.

I was so happy when I got home to find Didi getting better. Jen knew she had a decision to make and so did I. A friend of ours said that we could live with him, so we did. It was perfect for us. We didn't have to contend with all of the bullshit we had at our other place. After 90 days of going back and forth to the hospital and moving everything, we finally felt like a family.

It was getting real hot, too. I remember having to take Didi for walks after 1:00 in the morning because it was so hot. I think the summer of 1980 was one of the hottest on record at that time; it sure felt like it. It did not do much though to dampen our spirits; no, not at all.

There were still things that Jen didn't know at that time. She didn't know how much I loved her. She knew I loved Didi since the first time I set eyes on her. I loved both of them so much. I did not know if Jen knew that I loved her enough to stay with her. She told me that she thought she should go home and see that Didi got the care she needed. She said she loved me, but Didi's needs had to come first. I knew she was right. But, what she didn't know was how far I would go to do what it took to ensure that both of them would be mine. I couldn't blame her. I know that she needed actions, not words. She needed to believe that I meant what I said. The fact was that I had been selfish in the past. But that was before Didi was born. Jen was still thinking that one guy had already left her over a baby, why would I be any different.

So until she left we still did things together and had a great time. But it was coming to an end and we both knew it. She thought that I was going to re-up and stay in the air force, and I admit I had wanted to do just that. But after the bullshit in Iran, my thoughts were different.

By this time it was July and it was real hot still, and it was time for a going away party for my girls. I remember looking at Didi and those big beautiful brown eyes of hers, and thinking that I couldn't live without them. I did not want to do that. Didi was the belle of the ball. Everyone loved her. As we partied, I told Jen that I was going to marry her. She started to cry. I knew she didn't believe me.

She said, "I want to, but I…" She just stopped what she was saying and shook her head back and forth.

So I said it again in front of everyone. "Hey! Listen up everybody! Do you all think I love this woman?"

"Yes!" Everyone shouted.

It was too much for her. She was leaving what she had come to love. I knew then what I had to do.

Jen and Didi left two days later. I was crushed. My girls were gone, and I was lost for awhile. It came time for me to re-up. My heart was not in it. I did have a business to go home to. That was what I needed to do. That was my dream. It had taken my entire life to find my dream, and here it was. All I could think about was Jen and Didi, not the Air Force. I had served my country and it was time for a new direction in my life.

I still remember when I called Jen at her grandparent's house. Didi was crying in the background, and Jen couldn't get her to stop. I asked her to put the phone up to Didi's ear.

"Didi, it's Daddy," I said. It was sudden, total silence. Jen was shocked that Didi recognized my voice, and I continued. "Didi, you listen to Mom and go to sleep for her."

Before Jen hung up the phone, Didi was asleep. I believe that was the first time that Jen thought that I was going to keep my word. It was also when I told her that I was getting out and going home to Arkansas.

"Why?" she asked.

"Hell, woman, why do you think?"

She said, "I don't know A.J. You had it made. Didn't they offer you a job at AWACS?"

"Yes, but my heart belongs to someone else."

She said, "Who?"

"Damn, woman, who do you think?" I knew that she knew the answer to that question, but was too scared to believe it.

"I want you to be my wife," I told her. "Does that answer your question?"

She responded, "I will believe it when I see you get off that plane. Oh, and by the way, find out from the doctors out there the best place for Didi, as far as the care she needs."

"Okay, my love, okay."

That was the first time Jen started to believe that I meant what I said. I was sure of what I wanted for the first time in my life. All my life I had looked for a sign from God to tell me what I needed to do.

As it turned out, it was what I truly had dreamed of my whole life, and not just another fart in the wind type of thing. It was the dream of my life. It was a God thing. I told Jen when I got out and home, that I was either going to tell her I told you so, or the minute I got off the plane, I would stick out my tongue at her. I wanted her to know that the man she loved would not change for the worse, but be the husband and father that she always wanted. Jen wouldn't believe me until she saw me at the airport in Los Angeles.

The last few days in Texas were hard because it was the end of an era for me. We had a party from hell. About 150 people showed up. It was an unforgettable party. We had 150 rums in a watermelon, two kegs on the back porch, and we were all doing acid and smoking all the pot we could find. I think it took about three days to recover from that night, but it was a great time and the right way to say goodbye to the life I had come to love before I met Jen.

I had done all I could do for my country. They still could have me do things for them if they chose to do so, and they did just that, but not until I kept my promise to my ladies. I got my release papers and was on my way home, with one mission left. That mission was to go to California and get on my knees and ask Jen to marry me. That was the only thing that I was thinking about.

The drive home took about ten hours, and when I got to Conway I was happy to see my mom and dad. When I told them my plans, they both said that they knew my intentions. That took me by surprise because I wasn't sure they would go along with what I wanted to do. But, to my shock, they told me that they knew it when I called them when Didi was so sick and had a temp. They could tell by my voice that they knew what I was going to do. It was truly God doing for me what I could not do for myself. I had done just about every thing that a person could have done as far as the military was concerned. I had done things I was proud of and things that I was not proud of. But, I had done good things. The biggest thing I had done was to find a little peace in my life for the first time in a long time. I had no regrets. It was time to move on with my life. A new day had come to pass. Now it was time to move on from one way of life to another. I was sad, but hopeful that my choice was the right one. For the first time since I was young I had a dream that was unfolding right in front of my eyes.

CHAPTER 14
The Dream Comes True…At Least For Awhile

    It was strange not being in the military. It had been my life for quite awhile, and I had met numerous people and made lots of friends. I had learned a lot about how the world really was; a cold and bitter place outside our little towns and neighborhoods where we grew up. I knew my friendships that I had made were to be just a memory, and things would not be the same.
    Then there were my ladies. That was, at that time, the driving force in my life. It's all I thought about. I called Jen and told her that I was on my way home, and that I was coming to see her. She sounded excited and she said that if for some reason I didn't make it she would understand, being that I was young and there would be girls in Conway who would want a guy like me.
    I said to her, "Baby, you do not understand, do you?"
    She said, "What?"
    I said, "I am going to marry you Jennifer!"
    At first, she said nothing. Then she said, "You haven't said my real name in awhile!" She started to cry.
    "I told you I loved you, and only you! I will be there in a couple of days, and I will call you with my flight information."

She said she'd be there to pick me up.

I then went home and told my parents what I was going to do, and they said they knew a long time ago that I loved her and would be going to California when I got home from the military.

As I got on the plane all my thoughts were on Jen and Didi. I was so excited. I couldn't breathe at times. The flight took me to New Mexico, then on to L.A. When the plane started to prepare to land I could see just how big the city was. It was bigger than I thought as it just kept going and going until we landed. I thought it would never end. I got off the plane and didn't see Jen, but I didn't know how big of an airport it was. So I started to go to the baggage pickup and was just in awe at the amount of people there. Then I saw her. And as I promised, I stuck out my tongue. It was funny.

Jen's sister had told Jen how many weird people were in this airport, and she said, "Look at that one. He's a weird one."

Jen just laughed. She gave me a big hug and kiss, and laughed some more. She introduced me to her sister and told her sister the story about sticking my tongue out when I saw her. Then her sister got the joke. As we went to get my bags, Jen said the big test was coming next. I asked her what test she was talking about.

Jen said, "My grandparents. They are from Arkansas. They came out here a long time ago. If they like you, then you are home free."

I knew then we were going to get married. My focus shifted to Didi.

"How is Didi?"

"Oh, A.J., she is something else. I told her that you were coming and her face just lit up, Baby."

I could not wait to see her. So, as we drove to Jen's grandmother's house, I looked around at the sites that I had seen on TV as a child. They were all around me. I saw the Sunset Strip, Santa Monica Pier, and of course the ocean. Being from the South, it was like a dream. At first, it was overwhelming.

It took about an hour to get from LAX to Malibu where the grandparents lived. When we got there, I was nervous. Then I met them. They were good people. I liked them very much. I felt a little out of place because of my surroundings. That changed when Jen's grandfather, Boog, told me I needed a shave. It made Jen's day. I had not shaved since I had gotten out of the Air Force.

Then I heard Didi playing in the living room. She had not heard me yet.

I went into the living room and looked at her and said, "Is that my Didi?"

Her big brown eyes got bigger believe it or not, when she saw me. "Hey, little girl."

She started to crawl to me, and I almost broke down in joy.

It made her day and mine. I was with both of my ladies. It was a moment in my life that I will never forget.

I was having a great time. We went to Oxnard where Jen's dad lived. That's when I first encountered her brother, Jimmy. He was a little weird to say the least. He wanted to fight! I wouldn't fight him. I told him I didn't come to fight. He just kept on. Jen was trying to tell him to stop, but he wouldn't shut up. Well, I had enough. I told him I'd put my right arm behind my back just to make it even. He didn't know what to make of that. We started trying to hit each other, and I was bitch slapping him around. It was an unfair fight to begin with. Then he decided to put his hands in a fist and that did it. I beat the shit out of him with one hand still behind me. Finally, I just pushed him up against the wall and he fell knocking a lamp down as well.

Jen came in and slapped her brother up the side of his face saying, "Damn, Jimmy, the man is a fourth degree black belt. He will kill you, you dumb shit! If I can whip you, then what do you think he will do?"

After that we got along just fine. I thought to myself what a first day this was. The rest of the day was full of good times talking to her dad, brother, and sisters. I met two more members of her family and then we went back to her grandparents' house in Malibu. They were on their way to see some of their family that still lived in Arkansas. I think that they liked the way that I loved both Jen and Didi and the way I conducted myself. As we played with Didi in the living room it became apparent that what I wanted most of all was to be a father. Jen and I got high and fell madly in love all over again in the 30 plus days that I was there.

During that time, I got down on my knees and asked Jen to marry me. She said yes. The time I spent there with them was just a beginning to a wonderful love affair. Didi and I loved to play around and she was getting to know that I would never harm her. I would take care of her and her mother.

I called my parents and told them to get ready for a trip to southern California in December. We decided to get married on the 20th of that month. I was going to have to leave for awhile to take care of things in Arkansas and I didn't want that. I just wanted to wrap them both up and take them to Arkansas with me. But Jen wanted Didi to see her doctor in California to find out what the future held for our little girl.

When I got home Jen had called my parents to thank them for the chance to be part of my family. She wanted them to have me call her. So I called her when I got home, and she told me that the doctor said that she could not take Didi to any better place than Arkansas because of Arkansas Children's Hospital. He thought it was the best children's hospital in the country. We felt even better about Didi's future.

I asked my life-long friend, Ronnie Harvy, to be my best man, and Jen asked his wife to be her maid of honor. I found us a house and prepared it for my ladies to come to Arkansas. I was working at the nursing home that my family owned and things seemed to be going well, maybe too well at times. I was hoping for the long wait to come to an end. What it really was is that I missed them oh so much that at times I just walked around in a daze. Even though it was just over a month it seemed to be a life time, and I couldn't wait. I called during the Thanksgiving holiday and told Jen that I was getting to the point that I just wanted to take both her and Didi and go off to get married, but I knew that she and my mother would try to kill me if I even thought of it again. So I didn't bring it up again.

Finally, it was time for me to fly back out to California to get married to the most beautiful woman I had ever known. As I got on the plane I knew that it would be the last time I would be a single man again. All I could think was that being single was not what it was cracked up to be, and I couldn't wait to see them both.

It seemed to take forever for the plane to taxi up to the gate when we landed. When I finally got off the plane and saw Jen and Didi it made the long wait worth it! I felt a sense of humility and love. Jen's little sister, Sheri, had to kick me to wake me up! I didn't care. It was a time for Jen and me to wonder if this was too good to be true. Jen asked if maybe she was daydreaming. I told her that maybe we were both daydreaming. I think it was a perfect thing that brought us together.

I stayed with Jen's grandparents for a couple of days while the bride-to-be got her wedding dress ready. I loved her grandparents a lot. They both were great people. Even Jimmy and I got high together. It seemed like the party would never end. What a great time to get married. Jen and I chose the man who would marry us, and I knew that my mom would want him to shave his beard. That made a perfect joke to laugh about.

When Mom came out with Ronny and his wife, Jen and I picked them up from the airport. On the way I found a hit of acid in my wallet. Being the crazy guy that I was, I asked Jen if she wanted to half it with me. She did. I really think Jen thought it wouldn't do anything. I was dealing with Sheri.

A funny thing happened when we all went into the airport. Boog told me to just smack Sheri, Jen's sister, on the behind if she got out of hand. Well, Sheri tested me. She kicked me and yelled "rape" loud enough to get the attention of everyone around. So, I did what Boog said to do. I smacked her on her behind. It made her so mad. She kicked me again and yelled again. Jen thought it was funny, and finally, so did Sheri. I was starting to get off on the acid that I took. It wasn't affecting Jen. It all made for a funny evening.

My parents and Ronny and his wife got off the plane as I was really getting off. All the way home from the airport, Jen was holding her hand over her eyes because she couldn't believe this was happening. She couldn't believe I was tripping when my parents got to California, much less at her grandparents' house. This was all reminding me that this was where Bob Dylan did his Highway 61 album.

When we got home, Didi was almost asleep. Ronny and his wife and Jen were in the living room. My parents were with Boog and Erie in the kitchen talking. Another funny thing happened. Jen's grandmother asked if I was drunk. When Jen told her I wasn't drunk, she asked why I had my sunglasses on at midnight.

Jen came over to me and said, "What the hell do you think you are doing? You are playing backgammon with your sunglasses on and it's after midnight!"

"Oh, shit! It must be the acid!" I answered.

"Well, take them off!" Jen demanded almost in tears laughing as hard as she could.

It was a wonderful week of love and wedding bells for us all. The family was getting ready for the wedding, and Jimmy, Ronny, and I were getting high to calm my nerves. My dad said he thought we were all nervous and we needed a joke to calm us.

He proceeded to say, "This old Italian man wanted to know if his sons were good Italian sons so he asked them from the oldest to the youngest what food they liked. The oldest said he liked spaghetti. The man told him he was a good son. Then the middle son said he liked lasagna. The old man said he was a good son. The youngest son said he liked pussy. The old man said that pussy tasted like shit. The youngest said, but Dad, you take too big a bite!"

Well, I thought we were going to shit our pants.

Then my dad went into the room where my mom was doing Jen's hair and told them that I was high. My mom about fainted. So, Dad changed it and said he meant I was hyper.

Jen told me later that she thought she would never make it through the wedding because of the way my parents were making her laugh.

The time came for Jen to walk down the aisle. I stood there waiting. It was clear to me that this was where I was meant to be. Then I saw her in her wedding dress, and I had never seen anything so beautiful! I was the luckiest man in the world! I knew then that there was a God. As we looked into each others' eyes we knew that we were meant to be here at this moment in time, and the love in our hearts would be forever. It was the best thing we would ever do in our lives.

"Now I pronounce you man and wife!" Those words I had wanted to hear since the day I met Jen were finally spoken. I was married to a woman who was in love with me. That alone was overwhelming. And there was Didi. She was beautiful in her little dress.
We were the happiest couple in the world. My life was complete. We went to our room and Jen started crying. I asked her if she was okay.

She put her hand over my mouth and said, "Yes, just make love to me, my husband. Just make love to me!"

I did just that. We fell into each other's arms and slept.

The next morning, her brothers were waiting for us to come out so they could shower us with a song. It was the worst song in the world, but we felt happier at that moment than any other point in our short marriage.

We took Ronny and his wife and my parents to the airport to say goodbye for the time being. We would follow them the next day. We said our goodbyes later to Jen's family. It was sad for Jen and her grandparents. They had come to love Didi and me.

We went to the airport the next day to take the red eye to Dallas and then on to Little Rock. We got to the airport and found out that the plane couldn't take off because of the fog. We only had two bottles and three diapers for Didi. I kept asking the people at the counter if they knew when the plane would take off, and they said that it would depend on the fog. We finally took off the next morning at 6:30 and flew to Dallas. We ran to the gate to catch the plane to Little Rock. We just made it. On the flight, Didi started to cry and we could not get her to stop. We got a few looks from the people beside us, one lady in particular. Jen told her that if she had been stuck in an airport with a child this young without a bottle or a diaper, she wouldn't be looking at us like she was. The lady didn't stare at us anymore.

I said to Jen, "That's my baby."

It only took 50 minutes to get to Little Rock, and when we got there no one was there to pick us up. So I called my parents. They had been trying to find out where we were. They had been told by the airlines that we were still in Dallas. We told them what we had been through and that we were in bad need of some formula for Didi. They said they would be there as soon as they could.

While we waited, Jen asked, "Is this a private airfield?"

I laughed and answered, "No, this is Little Rock."

She was amazed that it was so small.

I said, "Yes, baby. But you are not in Kansas anymore."

She thought we were in some country place that didn't even have a McDonald's. It was funny at the time, but it was really funny when my parents got to the airport and my mom shared her story about marrying my dad. She had come from Scotland to Arkansas! It was also funny when we were on our way to Conway. Jen had a strange look on her face and I asked her what was wrong.

She answered, "Where are all the leaves? The trees are dying!"

"No, Baby. It's winter."

"You mean the trees don't have leaves in the winter?"

"Yes, but they will come back in the spring." I knew this would be a strange world for her; Arkansas in the wintertime.

We had a great Christmas because of the fact that for the first time I had my own family. It meant a lot to Jen, too. We also had our own house. That made it just all that much better. We were looking out the window of our new home on Christmas Day, and we both said at the same time that we did the right thing getting married.

New Year's Day arrived, and we were just happy to be together. We didn't celebrate because we had already done that when we got here. We put Didi to bed, and we went to bed ourselves. All of a sudden we heard people outside. It sounded like they were having a party outside my house. I thought it sounded a lot like my parents' voices. We looked outside the window and it was my parents. My dad started knocking on the door. Jen didn't want me to let them in. I told her that my dad would never stop until we opened the door so she put something on and we opened the door. They were tight to say the least.

They yelled, "Happy New Year! Let's get drunk!"

I told them to calm down because we had a baby asleep.

My dad yelled, "Hell, my son, we'll get her to party with us!"

I told him, "Hell, no. You both have fun. We are going back to sleep."

They left. Jen couldn't believe it. She didn't think they were like that at all. I told her that was the first time I'd ever seen them like that.

"Really?" Jen asked.

"I guess it's the fact that we are here and they thought we'd be up. It was obvious they had been to the country club."

That really was the first time I could ever remember them being that way.

A couple of weeks after that, it started snowing and Jen had never seen snow. It was really something. Didi just loved it. I was enjoying the times we were having together. It was still like a dream come true. Like all dreams, though, it was short lived.

After my parents left that New Year's Eve, Jen and I had made love. Later, Jen found out she was pregnant. I didn't think of it at the time, but Jen was worried that our new baby would have the same problems that Didi had.

So, we had all the tests one could have at that time to find out. The tests were all negative. We were happy that our new baby would be okay. But, Didi had to have more surgeries. It was a rough time for her and Jen, and I was worried about them both.

We found a bigger house and moved into it in February. It was out of town in a subdivision that had two acres with the houses. The neighbors were nice but not overly friendly, except the older couple across the street. Our house was a split level house with three bedrooms and a big den. We thought it was perfect for us at the time, and with a baby on the way it had a nice room to fix up for our new arrival.

Didi had about four more operations which made it tough on Jen and me. Jen was working with me at the nursing home as I prepared for my administrator test. I was taking correspondence courses through University of St. Louis. It was a happy, but hard time for Jen because I was working long hours and trying to help the best I could. With what Didi was going through, we seemed to never get enough sleep or time to really take rest from anything. It was life on life's terms everyday, and it was taking its toll on both of us.

Jen had stopped smoking, but I seemed to smoke more cigarettes and pot almost daily. I had some friends over once and Jen found a needle between the cushions of the couch later. She got mad. She thought I had put it there. It turned out to be a friend who had left it there, and I told him if I ever saw anything like that again, I would kill him right there and then. We didn't see him for a long time after that. I told Jen that I meant it when I said that that part of my life was over. I think she knew that, but still worried about it like I did. We had told each other that we would not have that life in our home ever.

At the same time the country was in a recession and interests rates were going through the roof. It was getting hard for a lot of people to make ends meet. The gas prices were getting higher and with that so did everything else.

Time grew near for the baby to come. Jen was still afraid something would go wrong with this baby. She would have to have a C-section because she had one when Didi was born. The closer it got to the baby coming the more stressful it got for both of us. Even though the doctors told us that mother and baby were fine, we were still worried.

The only good times we had were playing with Didi and having each other to hold. The love that we had for each other held us together and kept us from going crazy at times.

Work was getting harder, but the money we were making kept things much easier for us to do what we wanted for the house and for the baby's room. Jen was so proud of what she had picked for the colors and furniture in the room. I was very proud of my wife, and my love for her just got better and more satisfying. Raising a family is hard work, and just to get by wasn't enough for us.

The expectations of my parents were also hard to live up to. They demanded perfection on everything. I had a lot of studying to do all the time for my test to become an administrator, and even though I had the best teacher in the state, my dad, and he wanted more. He was going to get it or else. You see, I was to be nothing but the best at everything, and it was becoming a problem at work and at home. The life we had was very hard because of that fact.

The time was finally here for Jen to go in and have the baby, and of course the doctors said it was a boy so we planned on a boy. My uncle and aunt came all the way from Scotland to be here when the baby arrived.

At the hospital, I told Jen that I loved her. I was in the waiting room hoping for the best, and I got a call. God had the funniest way of telling me it was a girl after all. I went to the phone thinking it was strange to get a phone call here. I answered the phone and Jen was on the line.

She said, "Well, she is here!"

I said, "Jen, is that you?"

"Yes, she is here! While I'm the one having a baby, you are just sitting out there, so come in here!"

I knew then that God had a sense of humor. I walked into the room, and I saw Lilly for the first time. She was beautiful. Jen was not impressed because of the process she had just gone through. My family told me how proud they were and they were proud it was a girl. I didn't care as long as she was healthy. The thought that I had two girls didn't enter my mind. I loved the fact that I was a father most of all.

We took Lilly home a couple of days later and Jen was well enough to cook dinner for my aunt and uncle after a few more days. That was to be another one of those times that we both would never forget. You see, there is a tradition in Scotland about a greeting. That is to get a piece of bread and slap the host across the face with it. Well, Jen and I had made everything just perfect for my family to come eat at our house. Jen was looking forward to this since she knew that my uncle and aunt were coming. The table was set, and everyone was there and all of a sudden my uncle hit Jen with the bread. You would have thought that someone had broken her heart. She started to cry. My mother told her it was a compliment. Then she knew for sure our family was weird to say the least. It became a point to her that when we got the chance to go to Scotland, she was going to return the favor. As far as the dinner went, it was great.

Jen's brother came out to find a job and live with us for awhile. It turned out to be a problem because he was into everything known to man. Jen and I started to do some cocaine too, but not that much. I loved her so much that I didn't do the right thing and say no, but yes to what I knew in my heart would become a problem for us. By this time money was good and we were not saving for the future. Instead we were just putting it up our noses. Lilly was growing at a rate that we weren't used to because of Didi.

One night, Jen's brother took the car and didn't come home. I was really mad and Jen said she would handle this one. She wanted to kill him as well. When he got home, I saw a side of her that surprised me. Boy did she go off on him, and it wasn't long before he went back to California.

Before he left though, we caught him getting into our stuff. I thought it would teach him a lesson if I replaced our stuff with baking powder and had him do it. So I put a big line of the baking powder out for him and offered it to him. Well he came back and said he liked that. He said it was the best we had, and wanted some more. After that we both started calling him "Baking Soda". We and our friends laughed about that for awhile, but what we couldn't see was what we were doing to ourselves by doing cocaine.

I got a good price on a corner lot, and we started building a new house in town in a subdivision that was close to the nursing home. It was a good neighborhood. We also had a good winter and Jen and the girls played in the snow. It was a joy to watch. I remember those times and think of the pure joy we had as a family, and I wish I had them back. But as you know we can't turn back the clock.

We moved into the new house in February. We thought we had the world at our beckon call. We were setting ourselves up and could not see it.

Didi was going through the roughest time with her surgeries. It became hard to say no to the drugs. With work and going to the hospital all the time, we didn't think we could go on without it. We were getting in too deep, so much so that we were doing it at the hospital, too. I look back now and I know that was the time my addiction was so bad. I was doing about $1000 a day just to help me keep up with work and Didi and Lilly. Jen didn't think we had a problem, but it was our friends who told me that we were out of control. I don't think there was a day that we weren't doing it. The hospital and the doctors told us that Didi's heart had to be operated on within a year. That made us nervous about her future.

We would go to the park a lot, and they would watch me play basketball. I bought a 1946 juke box for Christmas, and the girls were loving that because I set it so they would have to put a quarter in it to play a song. That was also a way for them to save money. For me, it was a great time, but for Jen it was a time that her addiction was in full bloom. I started to see that she was changing and that she didn't want the kids around a lot. It was disheartening to us that she'd rather be alone than to be with us. So, I took the kids everywhere and loved it.

CHAPTER 15
The Nightmare Continues!   Nothing Changes; Nothing Changes

    I was working long hours and when I wasn't I was taking the girls with me. Being a father was the most important thing in my life at that time. It was, however, hard to figure Jen out because she didn't seem to want anything but to come home after work and just do cocaine and sleep. I know that she was worried about Didi, but Lilly was her child too, and it seemed that she just wasn't up to being a mother at times. What I couldn't see was what effect it was having on me. We had parties with about 40 to 50 guests. We'd have kegs of beer and pot and of course, lots of cocaine; thousands of dollars worth at one party. I came home one afternoon and found Lilly covered in cocaine.
    When I walked into the room she threw her arms up and shouted, "Hey Dad!!"
    I just went off and ripped Jen up for having the shit out where she could get into it. Jen just didn't find it to be that bad of a deal, and that was the first real sign that things were getting out of hand. But

like all people in active addiction, I didn't do anything different to stop the problem at hand. I just went on and on and on doing the same thing over and over again. Plus, I was getting jealous about anybody who even talked to Jen.

The doctors told us that Didi would need surgery on her heart soon. That was a shock to us because we had assumed it would be much later in her life before she needed it. But, we had to do it. It just seemed like a bad dream. Didi took it like a champ.

Didi said in her beautiful little voice, "Let's do it!"

She had such a will to live. It brought me hope that things would be okay. At the same time though, we were scared to death about it. We both did more drugs to cope with life on life's terms. We knew that was not the way parents should do. I will never forget that I, the father who was supposed to be the leader of this family, went to pay off the drug dealer the morning of Didi's surgery. Now that's being a real dad. Shit, I wasn't doing anything at that time to prove I was a father either.

The doctors had shown us some pictures of what it would be like when she came out of the operation, but nothing prepares you when it's your own child. It took nine and one-half hours to complete the surgery, and when Didi came out, I just cried and Jen fainted. I had no idea if she was alive or dead; that's how bad it looked.

The courage that little ball of strength showed was more than enough to go around for us all. I had seen courage like that in the military, on TV, and in stories, but I had never seen it in a little girl and probably never will again. The doctor who did the operation was from Boston, and the man sat by my daughter's bed for three days and nights, and only charged us $600. Now that's a doctor.

Boy, surgery was a miracle! Didi was up and running out of the hospital within a week. But, sad to say, her parents were up and running in an hour. That's not what the girls asked for or deserved. It had become a problem, and there were no blue skies to be seen in the near future, either.

After we knew that Didi and Lilly were okay, Jen and I had the opportunity to go to Scotland. It would prove to be the last time Jen and I would ever have a good time together without the children.

We had the time of our lives. Jen also got to get back at my uncle for hitting her with the bread. We went all over Edinburgh and other parts of Scotland, and for the most part we were enjoying each other for the first time in a while. I think if you were to ask both of us, we would say that it was our only true honeymoon. It also gave us a break from our active addiction, at least for a while. I think it was the last time we were, or seemed to be, madly in love with each other.

When we got back it was business as usual. Work was the same, taking care of the girls was the same, and our addiction was the same. I wanted to stop smoking. With all the drugs we were doing, we were both smoking too many cigarettes. The meth was doing a number on me, and the cocaine was doing its thing on Jen, and the girls were caught in the middle of it all.

One time my father told Jen that she had to go home because she didn't have enough makeup on. Well, she started to cry, and my dad, being the person he was, told us both to go home if we couldn't do as he wanted. As we were pulling out of the parking lot I thought to hell with this and pulled right back up to the nursing home, went inside, and asked him just what the hell he thought he was doing.

We started fighting. I had had enough, and I yelled, "What would you do if someone told my mother the same thing?"

He replied, "I'd knock the hell out of him!"

I said, "Well get ready to get your ass whipped!"

He backed off then. I was out of there. I was on edge to the point that I wouldn't put up with anything like that from anybody. He knew just how far he could go after that.

Didi was still having a lot of operations, and it seemed like she wasn't able to go for any length of time without having to have a transfusion, and that was worrisome to us. We never knew if she would ever get better, and our bills were piling up and our insurance was giving us trouble. They wanted to drop us.

We were at the hospital one day, and the doctor who was head of the clinic at that time asked us if we had Tefra Insurance. We didn't know about that. The doctor suggested we get it. We had to apply for everything that the state had to offer, and after we were denied all of that, as Didi was, then Tefra automatically went into effect. After that, we had no more bills. It even paid for her supplies.

Lilly, on the other hand, was in day school at this time and was growing up too fast for me. It seemed that time was just flying by at an alarming rate.

The employees knew that Jen and I had a problem, and they all told us that if we didn't stop it was going to be bad for us, but worse for the kids. I knew they were right, but for some reason I couldn't stop, and Jen couldn't either. She didn't even want to stop.

The next year was still much of the same. I knew that I had to do something, but I didn't know what to do or how to do it, or where to go to get it done.

It was shortly after that when Jen and I got into a big fight over little things. That was so out of character for us. One day, I planned a hunting trip. She said she was going to the club with the girls. It wasn't anything to me until she didn't come home that night. Then she wouldn't even tell me where she had been or anything about it. She acted like I was wrong to even ask her about it at all. I knew if the tables were turned she would have raised hell.

This became our life and the girls were in the middle of it all. I knew in the back of my mind that something wasn't right. She was acting just like Cathy had acted. I was not happy because the way it was playing out was way too familiar. When Jen and I were only friends, I had told her not to underestimate me. I do not forget things like this. I remembered everything Cathy had done to me and to herself in the process. I just could not believe that this was happening again with the one person that I truly loved and thought more of than anyone else.

By this time it was 1987, and we sat down and had a meeting of the minds, so to speak, on that very subject. Jen said that it was getting too much for her to not only love me, but also work with me as she did. That made sense to me. The way my father thought when it came to the business was too much for her. He thought it was the company first and all the rest last.

I asked her how were we going to stop doing all the drugs, and it bothered me that I really didn't get a good answer to that question at that time. Maybe I was saying it wrong, or it was just me over reacting. I didn't know. All I did know was we had to stop. I was so stressed about it that all I was doing was getting high. Most of our friends didn't come around anymore, and that bothered me. It was a time for reflection of how our life had been.

I just lived in the past. I loved the times with the kids. I loved being a father. I remembered the time we took the kids to Boston to see Jen's sister. I remembered walking the kids down 42street and looking up at all the buildings. I remembered the day Lilly was baptized and she kicked me in the nuts right in front of the whole church. Everyone burst wide open with laughter, and I had to just stand there and take it. Looking back it was very funny, but at the time I couldn't do anything but hurt like hell. I remembered the times we held each other and just loved being together. We had a great life and were throwing it all away because of the drugs.

I was thinking about those things the day I had a gun in my hand. It was the same morning that Jen and my mother went to the doctor to see if Jen was pregnant again. I was just too high to care. I wondered how it would feel to shoot myself in the leg. I was so high that when I pulled the trigger, I didn't even feel it hit me. So I got up and locked the door and drove to work thinking that I had missed. By the time I crossed the railroad tracks close to work, I knew that I in fact didn't miss. I began to be in pain. When I got to the nursing home, I was in so much pain I told the activity director to go and get my dad.

"What happened?" she screamed.

I told her I had accidently shot myself.

As Dad drove me to the hospital, he told me to look up. Then he slapped me across the face.

I screamed, "What the hell are you doing?"

He replied, "You are in shock. You are hyperventilating!"

I told him, "Hell! I am in pain, you shit!"

He drove a little more and slapped me again.

I said, "Hell! If you do that again…"

Out of nowhere, he hit me again.

I said, "Damn, Man! I'm in pain, you son of a bitch!"

We got to the hospital, and I started to walk around the car to knock the hell out of him, but the nurses came out. They got me to the room so the doctor could look at my knee. Then a cop came in and asked me what happened. I told him that we had a peeping tom the night before and I slipped on a wet towel and the gun just went off. He bought that idea, and went about his business.

My dad asked me if I wanted to stay there or go to a Little Rock hospital. I chose Little Rock, so he called my mom. She was worried about me of course. She and Jen were just leaving the doctor. I knew she was pregnant because I was the one who always had the morning sickness.

Mom asked Jen if she wanted to sit down. Then Jen asked my mom if she wanted to sit down. Jen told my mom that she was pregnant. My mom responded by telling Jen that I shot myself.

Well, I can only think of what Jen was thinking because my dad didn't tell my mom where I had shot myself. Jen, I am sure, wanted to know how I was, so they met us at the hospital in Little Rock. As best as I can remember they got there about the time I was coming off of the drugs I had been given.

I looked up and saw them and then I noticed that blood was shooting out of my knee. All I remember saying was I didn't want a fucking thing to go wrong. Then I went out again. When I awoke I was in the operating room asking the doctor how bad it was. Then I woke up in the room and Jen was crying.

"Why, A.J.? Why?" Jen asked.

All I could or would say was, "I slipped!"

It took years before I would tell the truth about what I had done that morning. I was in pain alright, but it wasn't my knee that was hurting. It was every part of me; my heart, mind, and soul were in pain. After we got home, all my friends joked about how good a shot I was. Well, if they only knew.

Jen wasn't happy at all that she was pregnant. We talked about it and she acted like she didn't want another child. It made me wonder if it wasn't mine. I knew in my heart it was, though.

Didi still had operation after operation, and more and more transfusions. One time she went just two weeks before she had to have another one. She kept fighting and kept proving the doctors wrong about her outlook. It was a thing of beauty to watch this little girl go on with her life, and at the same time keep her sister in check.

Lilly was asked to do a lot for a young child. It wasn't her fault that Didi had all the family and friends telling her how good her sister was. She was a great little girl in her own right and had to do things that normal 6 year old girls didn't have to do. To her credit she didn't complain much, and she loved her older sister very much. They both were good kids.

I was always working or at the hospital with Didi, and Lilly just couldn't stay at home. She wanted to be with her sister and I was always proud of that. She also had a close friend, and they were two peas in a pod. In fact, they still are to this day.

It was November and time for Jen to have the baby. The doctors had told Jen that she wouldn't be able to have anymore children because of her previous C-sections, and that had seemed fine with her. I couldn't blame her either after what she had been through. But, here she was in the operating room again. We still didn't know what the baby was. I just knew it had to be a girl because I didn't think God would let us have a boy. I just knew it.

My parents kept the girls and I was at Jen's side. I saw parts of her I never want to see again. Then I got to hold my new daughter. She was beautiful. We named her Catie. Life seemed worth living again, at least to me.

Jen on the other hand was great at first, but as time went on it became clear that there was something wrong. I guess today they call it the baby blues, but with her it was much more. She had female problems.

We went on a trip to Mexico a couple of months after Catie was born to get away for a while and to find each other again. It almost turned out to be a terrible thing because one night Jen wasn't feeling well, and she told me to stay at the bar and have fun. When I got back to the room, she was asleep. I went to the bathroom and passed out on the toilet. When Jen got up, I remember looking up at her to see her bleeding badly. I called a doctor. He said I needed to get her home. He knew Jen had a bad problem that needed special attention.

CHAPTER 16
The Fall From Love to Hate

The doctor was right. The rough times were upon us all. The dark side was here, and it would become the way to the end of beauty. I could only hope that Jen was going to be okay. All I could do was to pray and do what I needed to do for all of us in this time of pain. I had to work not only for Jen and the kids, but for our love for each other. She had to have an operation as soon as possible. I was very worried about her.

Just two days after we got back she had the operation. I knew that it would be a long time before she would feel like herself again. I just wanted my wife back. I took it as my problem to try to take care of us all, and to work as much as possible to make sure that everything went as smoothly as possible during this period.

I was waiting on the doctor to come out of the operating room to tell me how the operation went. I was thinking about how I could be not only a better husband and father, but a better person altogether.

Just then, the doctor came out and said, "Well, your wife had a lot of problems, but I think we did the best that we could."

"What do you mean, Doc?" I said.

He replied, "We had to do a hysterectomy, and she is resting now."

I asked what I could do for her, and he told me to be very supportive and keep in mind that women tend to have some depression with this kind of operation. I had no idea that it was such a big deal, but I was going to find out what I could do for her and do it! Hell! I loved her! I didn't want to be like so many men and think well, she isn't a woman now. I think that if you truly love someone, then you will do what it takes to do the right thing. You will do all that you can to make things easy for your loved one.

But, Jen was never the same after that. It completely changed her in every way. The person that I had fallen in love with was gone after that never to return. The kids and I were never the same either. Our lives were changed forever.

Jen was already in depression and she just was not the same person that I grew to love. She went crazy, and I mean crazy! It became difficult for her to even look at the kids and me. It was as if we were the last thing she wanted or needed at this time.

I talked to so many doctors and people who had been through this, and they all said the same thing. They said she needed to be on hormones. But she refused to take them, and I think it drove her nuts.

The children didn't know what was wrong, and neither did I. She became cold and hateful, as if she was a totally different person. We were not a priority in her life.

I found myself crying at work, in the shower, and with the kids. They cried a lot, too. We all needed each other so much. It was heartbraking to us all. We were lost, and the worse it got, the more drugs I took to ease the pain of it all. At the same time, I held the kids close to me because none of us knew what to do but hold each other as tight as we could to try to stop the pain of seeing her do this to herself and to us.

This time was so painful to all of us because we didn't know what was happening. The girls would just cry for their mother, and I just kept telling them that it would all be okay and that mom had to go through this on her own. I was sure to tell them it wasn't their fault. They would just cry themselves to sleep. They were sleeping with me at that time.

What hurt me the most was them telling me to tell mom they were sorry because they thought it was something that they had done. When they would finally go to sleep I just prayed to God to give them some hope that their mother would come home and I prayed to keep them from thinking that it was somehow their fault. It was hard to see them go through this, but it was especially hard to know they thought that way. That was making me hurt that much more.

When Jen would come home the kids would just hold her and would not want to let go. I would ask her to please think about what this was doing to the children.

She would curse me up and down like a dog, and say, "You are just a pet for your parents. All of it is your fault anyway!"

That just went all over me, and I tried really hard not to get into it with her. But, I was getting to the end of my rope, and we would fight about it. Hell! I was still a man, and I loved her dearly. I just didn't know what I had done that was so wrong.

I kept thinking that it must be my fault, and then I started questioning myself. Maybe it was my fault. It was hard on all of us, and I really think that with the drugs and what she had gone through that she didn't even realize what she was really feeling.

I kept on doing more drugs and holding the girls as long as I could. I wanted to keep them from feeling the pain as best I could. Didi was the strong one because of her problems. She was the oldest, and she was my rock. Lilly and Catie were hurting too, but they looked up to Didi and me for guidance.

I would try to block it out with drugs. I would go to the local Wal-Mart and cash big checks that were as much as $10,000. I'd have to spend 25 percent of it to get the rest in cash to keep my habit going. I thought I needed it to stay up for the kids. I thought it was helping, but in turn it was just putting me deeper into my addiction. It was not helping at all.

I remember one time at work we were having an argument. The employees knew what was going on and sadly they took sides. That was not a place for a soap opera. It was a nursing home where the patients had to come first. Looking back, I think we did well at putting them first, but it could have been a big problem.

I remember coming to work and having employees tell me to take care of what was on my nose. That was hard, to say the least. It wasn't a good time or a good way to help a problem at all. I was dropping the ball and I knew it.

I also remember the mad fits we would have that were tearing the kids and the family apart. I knew that I had to find help for my addiction; I had to try and find a way to solve my problem.

I remember one of those nights that Jen was home. We had come together for a moment and then we just went to sleep and didn't talk anymore. The next day my dad sat me down and asked me what was going on.

I answered, "Dad, I have a problem."

"What is it?" he asked.

"It is cocaine, dad. I have a cocaine problem and I do not know what to do!"

"Well, I think you better fix it, my son, because you are better at this job than you have been showing me."

It wasn't long before Jen came home again from one of her weeks out and we made love. Later, I was sitting in front of the TV. Before I knew it, I was coming out of a cocaine black-out, and to my surprise, I was at the Little Rock Airport with tickets to New York City, St. Louis, Denver, and San Francisco. I didn't know where I was or where the hell I was going. I then drove to a restaurant in the western part of Little Rock. I didn't know what time it was or what to do. I remember wondering what the hell was going on. I wondered if it was the drugs or God. It was both. God was trying to tell me something, and the drugs were just fueling the fire of the confusion of my addiction. It was as if the devil was handling the controls of a video game, and I was the visiting team that was losing badly. And the devil loved every minute of it.

So I got up and went to the pay phone back by the bathroom. I was looking through the phone book and came across an ad about rehabs. I called a place called Bridgeway.

Someone answered and I asked them if they had an "A.J. Shaw" in there.

They responded by saying they weren't permitted to give out that information.

I replied, "Well, you are going to have him soon!"

I found a rehab doctor in the phone book, and called her. Her office was not far, so I went over there as quickly as I could. She told me that I needed to go to Bridgeway immediately.

I called my dad, then Jen. The conversation with Jen was one that I will never forget.

After I told her, she screamed, "What! I will never forgive you for this, A.J.! I cannot believe you are doing this to me!"

Her words will be in my mind forever. I told her, "Doing to you! I have a problem, as you do. This is about me and our girls' lives. Not about you! I cannot believe what I am hearing come out of your mouth!"

So I hung up on her, and I went to Bridgeway. When I got there it was like I had come into a mental ward. I was so high that they gave me a shot and I went to sleep. As I slept, I dreamed of all the things I had gone through that year.

In April, I had TMJ so bad the doctor pulled all my teeth so I wouldn't get bad headaches. In August, I found out that I had to have a gall bladder operation and I almost died. My addiction was destroying my body. It seemed like I had only been asleep for a few hours when I awoke, but it had really been three days. They told me that they had estimated that I had so much drugs in me it should have killed me.

Damn! I didn't think I was doing that much!

Life does that to you when you are in active addiction.

At rehab, they wanted me to stop killing myself with worry about my job, the kids, and Jen. They told me if I didn't take care of myself, then it was a foregone conclusion that I would be dead and it wouldn't matter anyway. I had to do this for me, and me alone or I would die.

It took a while for me to get the idea of what they were trying to tell me, because my mind was on the girls and Jen. And, of course, what would people think if they knew that I had a problem. Yeah, right! Hell! Everyone knew anyway. I was the last one to know that I had a problem.

They brought me in with the group for the first time, and I was a little confused about how these people who didn't know me at all were going to help me. The other people in the group seemed to be just as fucked up as I was, and they showed me nothing that would make me think otherwise.

I was shown my room that I would be in and what, where, and how I was to act. I started to think that I had made a big mistake in coming here, but it was better than living the way I had been living. That surely wasn't working at all. In the group, there were about ten of us and we all started the day with a meditation. It was different to say the least.

I thought to myself, "Self, what the hell have I got to lose but everything, so why don't you get the fuck out of here now!"

"Sit down, A.J.!" said a black lady named Gladys.

I thought, "Who are you, bitch?"

But, I didn't say anything, and I sat down in one of the chairs and just listened to everyone tell me their names, and what they were there for. Most of them were strange, but I sat there and let them do their thing. I just wanted to go back to my room and get some more shit so I could go back to sleep. But it wasn't that simple. I had to say a little something about myself. Yeah, right!

"Hi! My name is A.J. I am a father of three girls, and I think I have a problem with…"

The lady interrupted and said, "So, you don't think you are an addict? You are going to be a challenge, A.J."

I thought to myself again, "You better get the hell out of here now, and I mean now. Get up! Get the fuck up now, boy!"

Then a thought came to me. I thought, they drugged me and really I am having a dream that the lady is the preacher in Jacksonville taking me back to that cop and they are forcing me into the church camp from hell and the cop is really the black lady in drag. He's got a gun, and he's going to kill me! These people are trying to keep me here! And, you know as well as I do that Jen has great pussy, and so what if she fucked everyone I know and some I didn't know.

Again, I told myself to go back to the room, have them give me more of what they gave me when I got here, and I'll wake up at home in front of my TV, and it will all be over!

But it was not a dream at all, and they were here with me to save me from myself. The rest of the day got worse. I didn't think I needed to be there at all. I got to thinking the doctor was really one of Jen's boyfriends trying to prove to everyone that I was the one that was going crazy, and it was her plan to take the girls away from me and that's why I was in this place to begin with because it was her that put something in my coca-cola to make me believe that I was in some funny farm and she was going to run off with the kids while I was here! Yeah! That was it! That was a cry for help for anybody that could hear me.

The thoughts that were going through my head continued throughout the night. They would not stop! I had gone insane, and the more I fought it, the stronger the nightmare that had driven me to this point became. I had no feelings at all. I didn't know what was real and what wasn't. I thought that someone should kill me now so I could be given an honest funeral. At least no one would think it was an accident. Or, was I already dead and didn't know it?

The next day, we met together again. The group was an interesting one. There was a big-time lawyer, and there was a lady that looked like one of those life long drinkers that would close down the bar and then go home with the cat if they would buy her a drink on the way out the door. And, there were a lot of people just like me. And just like me, they thought they could slide through rehab and not be noticed, and then go home and everything would be fine. Well, it does not work that way, and it took a while before I could see that I did have an addiction problem, not a moral one, and if I wanted to do so, I could stop, one day at a time.

My dad didn't see it that way though. He brought the girls to see me. They were as glad to see me as much as I was glad to see them. I loved my girls. The problem was that I didn't love myself. My dad thought that he had earned the right to do what he wanted to do and that no one had the right to tell him otherwise. As one of my friends once put it, there is a special place in hell for Mr. Shaw!!!

Things were going good, and I had been in rehab about two weeks when Jen came to visit me. That wasn't good and I knew deep inside my heart that our marriage was over. But, I still couldn't accept it.

One day, our group went to an AA meeting in Little Rock. I will never forget this guy that was outside the building where they met. He was smoking a joint and he took something like a xanax. Then he went into the meeting and said that he had 18 years sober. I knew then that place was not for me at all. I didn't know at the time that it was me that was holding me back. The people at Bridgeway knew it, though. They also knew that I wanted to go home to my kids before the holidays.

I had been there about four weeks when they let me go home. I loved being home with the kids, but Jen and I were not saying much to each other and that was bothering me. You could see that it had an effect on the kids, too.

It was good for me to get to go to an NA meeting in Conway. It was a small meeting with only about five or six people there. One of them was a guy that I had gotten high with before. He was a good friend of mine, but we'd been out of touch because he had been clean when I was just going wild in my addiction. His name was Joseph, but we had always called him "Dog". It was good to see him doing well. He told me that this wasn't going to be easy, but he thought I could do it if I wanted it bad enough. That was the problem. I did want it, but I was still closed minded about many things that I had to change. And at that point I didn't know what or how to change.

I knew there were some particular things I had to change, but in my mind, I thought I couldn't change those things. I got a sponsor, and I really did not like what he did at my house. He told me what I, or we, meaning Jen and I, had to do with the items in the house, like the booze Jen had in the cabinet. That just got Jen off on the same tangent.

She would make comments to me like, "You go ahead with your clean bullshit, and I will go get a guy who will fuck my brains out and you can go to hell!!!"

She said this in front of the girls, and that was hard on them. It was pretty clear that she didn't care at all what she said. The girls and I would sleep through the night; they would hold me all night and continue to tell me to tell Mommy they were sorry. That was one of the hardest things that I would go through because they still thought it had something to do with them.

I thought it was me. I thought I must have done something wrong to make her hate me badly enough to say those things. I would think absurd thoughts like my dick wasn't long enough, or it must be that I had all my teeth pulled, or I wasn't making enough money. I thought I just was not good enough to make her happy. That is the way that the addiction works. It makes things seem more than what they really are. The real problem with Jen was Jen. It wasn't me. It was her, and I could not see that because of my low opinion I had about myself. It would get to be an even bigger problem for me in the future.

The girls felt it more. I thought I could save them, when in fact I could not even save myself. The girls and I held each other closer than ever as Jen went through her addiction shortcomings. We just went through the motions as we had done for the last couple of years. Jen became more close-minded to the fact that she had turned away from us. We couldn't handle that at all. It hurt us, but the big thing was that it undermined my getting clean.

So I started getting high again, and this time it was worse than before in many ways. I could not get anything out of my mind except how I had fucked up everyone's life, and I just knew I was a failure. I got high to forget about everything. It was a long time before I thought that I could do anything right.

Jen, on the other hand, did everything she wanted, and the kids continued to feel like it was their fault. That hurt me the most. It just wasn't fair that these great kids thought that. I still remember the way Didi took over in the absence of parents who weren't there for her or the sisters that she loved so much.

It was a crime, yes, a crime. I was just as guilty as their mother was because I didn't stand up for what needed to be done for myself, much less these precious children. I took Jen back many times, and it became harder for the children to accept what she was doing to all of us.

Jen got even worse at doing what she said she would, and it made the children doubt her even more and hang on to me more. As my children cried, I saw that I had become a prisoner in my self-made prison. The jail was my illusion, confusion, and betrayal. We were all hypnotized by it and controlled by it, as the disdain became our cell. We were trapped by the dream of life without tears, without holes in the lies of the words of others that were controlling the keys to this cell of existence.

It would turn out to be my undoing to take her back again. My wish was for my love. But I had lost her to the unforgiving disease that turned the love we had for each other into a snowball from hell rolling out of control towards a hopeless conclusion. We tried again. At least, I thought we did. But, life would rear its ugly head when Didi was in the hospital again.

I had enough listening to the children cry, and I filed for divorce. I thought that the girls needed to be with their mother because they were girls, and they wanted to stay in their house, too. So I arranged it so Jen would keep the kids in the house, and I would live nearby to see that they were taken care of like they needed to be. It was a long drawn out affair. Jen thought that she would get a part of the business, but my parents and I saw fit that Jen would get nothing more than what I told her she would get. That would be a house with the kids. I would pay the bills, and the kids would be as happy as possible. I was wrong to think that Jen would take care of the girls that way. She had a different agenda.

Jen hired a lady that would help see after the girls, and in the meantime, she would run wild. She would do whatever she wanted and that was to party, party, and party some more. It would be her undoing. I thought I kept my eyes on the girls in my townhouse a block or two away, but there were things going on that were hidden without my knowing.

One weekend my dad and I were in Dallas at the Southwest Conference basketball tournament. It was the last time Arkansas was in the conference because the next year they were going to be a part of the SEC. I called Jen and asked her if I could come by on the way home and stay the night so I could take the girls to school the next morning. She said I could, but she had something else in mind. My dad advised me to just go home with him seeing that it would be late when we got back to Conway, and I said no. He told me he sure hoped I knew what I was doing. I told him I'd be okay.

He dropped me off at my car, and I went by the house. When I got there the back door was locked. I knocked, but no one answered. I could see the lights from our 1946 juke box reflecting through the living room window. So, I walked around the house to see if I could determine if they were home or not. Then I saw something that maddened me so much I wanted to fight. My so called ex-wife was being kissed by some guy on my couch. But, that is not what I got so mad about since she had been with a few guys since we had been together. What made me so mad was my three-year-old daughter sitting at their feet. I tapped on the window, and Jen saw something that she had forgotten about. That was my temper. This guy was about 6 feet 5 and around 270 pounds, but that never stopped me before, and she knew it wouldn't stop me this time.

She opened the door and shouted, "No! Do not start something, A.J.!"

The guy was sitting at the dinner table in the eating area by this time. Before he knew it, I hit him so hard that blood hit the wall behind him.

Jen went crazy and was shouting, "Look what you have done!!!"

I looked into the guy's eyes. They weren't just bloody, but they were fixed in such a way that they would never be the same again.

I said, "Boy, you don't want to piss me off, Boy!!! I will kill you, Boy, I will kill you!!!"

I guess Jen had forgotten what I had been through in my life. She did not know by asking both this guy and me to come by at the same time that she had released the demon inside of me again. The guy was in bad shape. He was lucky that I hadn't killed him, not for the fact that he was messing with Jen, but for doing it in front of, or should I say almost on top of my daughter. I went to my place and went to sleep. I knew that I had hurt the boy pretty badly. I thought the cops would be coming by and that I would probably be in jail soon. But, to my surprise that did not happen.

I was thinking that maybe my dad was right, but on the other hand I was glad that I saw it so it wouldn't happen again.

I got up the next morning and was going to work when I thought to myself, "Damn! What did I do?"

I got to work and everything was okay, I thought. It was a regular Monday morning until I saw a woman with an officer from the sheriff's department come in and ask for me.

My dad asked why they were there, and told him I'd handle it.

The lady looked at me and said, "You must have done martial arts on my son!"

"I just hit him one time. If I'd used martial arts on him, you'd be burying him. Your son was at the wrong place with the wrong person!"

My dad asked me what had happened and I told him. He told Mom and they went to see if the girls were okay. I wasn't supposed to go there for awhile, so Mom and Dad had to go check. I just wanted the kids to be okay. I wanted to make sure they were in the right place.

Things like that continued. I am sure, for the kids, it seemed like it would not end. At least I was a grown person. My girls were so small to have to be going through such a time. I am sure it felt like eternity to them.

I couldn't get a grip on anything, and I continued to get higher as the days went by. I just had monkey after monkey on my back. I felt more alone. It wasn't until my parents told me something had to change that it did.

Jen wanted to get back together. She had a new boyfriend, but then she found out he was worse than she thought I was. I was going crazier as each day passed. I had the kids every other weekend. The girls seemed more nervous than before. I couldn't put a finger on it, though.

Then, one day Jen came by my townhouse and said, "Listen, Johnny is going to hurt you because of the girls."

I said, "What do you mean because of the girls?"

She answered, "He is a mafia type and is connected to some bad people."

Now, that's just what I wanted my kids to be a part of.

It wasn't too long after that I got a call from a guy who said that he was nationwide and I needed to quit telling the kids that I was going to take them away from their mother.

I responded, "Man, if you want to meet me somewhere and keep your dad's boys away, then we will see who comes out!"

That was that. I didn't hear much more until about two weeks later. The lady who was keeping the girls in the daytime called me and asked me to come over.

When I got to the house I saw something that I never thought I'd see. There were pizza boxes all over the house, and she told me that she had not been paid in over a month, and that she would have been gone already if not for the fact that she loved the girls. She said the girls were scared to death. She said that Jen and this man had told her that if she ever said anything to me that he would kill the girls and put the blame on her, so she better keep her mouth shut.

I asked her how long it had been since Jen had been home, and she said it had been at lest 45 to 50 days since the girls had seen their mother. I could hardly hold my tongue, and I about cried myself to death thinking that I had them every other weekend and they had never said a word about that or about the way they had been treated.

I gave her some money and asked her to stay. I told her I would come over the next morning because I wanted to get to the bottom of this as soon as I could. She said she would stay and that she would be in touch as soon as I called her if I needed her. I told her I would be back after the kids went to school. I went back to the house and could not sleep or think clearly at all. I was so ashamed and mad at not only Jen but myself for not seeing what was really going on.

As soon as I could, I called my parents and my lawyer and started the paperwork to take full custody of the girls. I got a statement from the lady and a couple of other people.

Then I found out something that put a chill right through me. Lilly said to me that Jen and her boyfriend had told her and Didi that if they told me anything, I'd come and cut Jen's fingers off joint by joint. How could anybody say this to their own children? I was shocked, and when Didi said it was true, I knew what I had to do.

I tried to get a hold of Jen, but to no avail. When my lawyer had the papers ready we called the boyfriend and Jen answered.

I told her, "You have minutes to come down to the lawyer's office and sign over all rights to the girls and everything else including the house. If you don't, my lawyer will take this to the judge and you'll be charged with everything from neglect to attempted murder. You only have minutes, or else…"

I left so I wouldn't see them. I was afraid I would kill them both. For the first time I hated her. I couldn't think of anything else but the harm she had done to her own children. It consumed me.

The lawyer called me at my parents' house shortly after and said Jen had been there and signed everything. Of course, I went and got high just as I always did when anything like this happened. Nothing like this, though, had ever happened, and I just couldn't handle it. It was unthinkable to me that any mother would let this go on.

I went to Little Rock as the kids were with my parents. I knew they were safe, but I was still on the path to hell myself and couldn't see it yet. The friends I joined were just like me; high. It was just unnerving to think of this as anything but unholy.

The family that I once thought would last forever was no more. The country that I thought was the greatest in the world had become nothing but greed, power, and control. Drugs and murder were everywhere, and the world that I once thought of as beautifull had become evil, with no real end in sight. I was ashamed of it all, for I was as guilty as everyone else that had succumed to its hypnotizing hold on us all. Where I once saw beauty, I now saw hate. Where I once saw compassion, I now saw comtempt.

I had lost faith in everything but the love for three girls in the middle of it all. The world had forgotten about the future of these children that would have to carry the burden of our mistakes for the rest of their lives. I was scared for them. All the children of this so called world would be in the hands of the adults who were filled with unforgiving hatred for one another and for drugs, greed, money, power, and control. Shit! Like we gave a damn about them. It was like being trapped by our own self-seeking, self-centered gains that only produced hate, fear, and death for them all. We had all become puppets in a bad play and the world did not know what we were playing much less why. We didn't know who we were fighting nor for what. Only one word said it all, "Sad".

It was a while before Jen and I would see each other, much less talk to each other. I now had the girls all to myself. It was a good thing for us to be together again, at least for a while. For now the girls were happy with me and that in itself was a miracle. It was also nice to be back in the house that the girls were raised in, but it was also bittersweet because of that fact that it was also the house of pain for me.

It wasn't long before Jen called to ask for help to get away from the guy because he was treating her badly. So bad in fact that she was scared for her life. Shewas in trouble and I felt helpless. If I tried to help her, that would mean putting the girls in harms way again. The drugs were as they had been in the past a problem for me. It was getting worse instead of better, and I couldn't seem to shake it.

The girls just wanted to be free of all that. They still wanted to see their mother, but they wanted us to be together. I told them that would be hard because of what we had been through.

I was going to Little Rock a lot with my new friends and they were all doing meth and coke. That was right up my alley. I guess it was just my self-deception about using that clouded my thinking on how bad my addiction had become.

Otherwise, to me, things seemed to be going well. I was dating a nurse named Mary who worked for me at the nursing home. Mary got pregnant and I asked her to marry me. She said no. It seemed that everyone around me could see what I had become, but I couldn't see it. That didn't change the fact that I had another beautiful baby girl, Sydney, and my girls loved her, too. She was a big ball of joy that would become part of my life in the future, but for now her mother took her to live in Washington. I didn't know at that time if I'd ever see her again. I don't blame Mary, but it would have been nice to see Sydney more. My parents didn't believe she was mine, and they wouldn't accept her as their granddaughter. They still to this day do not think of her as their grandchild. I think that's bullshit, but I cannot change them.

I flew to Washington to see Sydney and Mary. It was a great time that I will remember always. The girls loved their little sister, and they were hoping it would not be long before they could see her again.

With Mary gone, it left a door open for Jen to return. She did come back for a little stay, and it all started again. Of course, I was still in love with a dream that was no longer there. The lies and doubts became the nightmare all over again. Jen, as always, thought she could outsmart me and get what she wanted, and she almost did. My thoughts were on my new baby, not Jen. As for me, I still had to go through a period when I was caught in the web of my addiction that seemed to never end, and I didn't know it at the time, but it was going to get worse.

Jen and I were back and forth; fussing and fighting one day, and caring about each other the next. It was difficult for the kids to handle. That, I think, was my fault because I let Jen come back only to leave again and again without a thought of the effect it had on the girls. Also, not knowing if Mary and my new baby were okay was hard on everyone except Jen. She couldn't care less.

So, I asked my parents if I could sell the part of my business to them for the chance to get back with Jen and make a new start in Nevada with the girls. They reluctantly said yes. In the back of my mind it semed like a dream that was doomed to failure, so my parents and I arranged things so I could buy the ownership back within six months if I decided to come back. I kept that part from Jen because I still had the kids to think about. In the back of my mind, I also thought it would be a good way to keep Jen from getting one over on me. It proved to be the best thing that I had thought of in a long time. I am convinced it was God doing for me what I could not do for myself.

Before we left for Nevada, our plan to move was tested by Jen's lack of thought for anybody but herself. Didi was in the hospital, and I had been there all night. I had some work that I had to do the next morning. Jen was going to the hospital in the daytime. It was about 2:00 in the afternoon when the hospital called and asked if I would bring some clothes for Didi. I said that her mother was supposed to be there with some clothes already, but they said that she had not been there at all. I couldn't believe it. Our daughter was there alone. Her mother had not been there at all. As the day went on it became apparent that Jen was nowhere to be found. I was, to say the least, very mad and hurt at the same time. Didi did not need to be in the hospital without any clothes, or without her mother there at her side. When the girls got out of school, and I knew Didi was okay, I started a quest to find Jen.

A friend of mine knew I was in a bad way. He knew I was going to hurt someone, so he offered to hunt for Jen for me. But I told him it was my job and no one was going to leave my daughter alone in the hospital and go off somewhere without paying the price for it. Catie and Lilly were mad because of the way their sister was treated by Jen. I started looking.

I didn't even know where to start looking. I was angry about the way Jen handled Didi especially just before we were going to Nevada. I had so many emotions going through me I didn't know what I'd do if I found her at all. I knew it would be like trying to find a needle in a haystack. I even thought maybe she'd been taken. Hell, I didn't know what to think.

I went to the guy who I got my drugs from, and I got some drugs from him to calm me down, if that was even possible. It was near midnight and the girls were asleep. I was calling everyone I could think of to find out anything about her or where she might be. I made two or three trips to my drug man by the time I got wind of where she might be.

Around 2:00 a.m. a friend thought he had seen the car at a low class motel in Conway. I went to the motel, and sure enough, there was my car. I stood there wondering just how I would handle the situation. It came to me that this was the turning point I was looking for that would make up my mind to go to Nevada with a purpose. It was as if God had made up my mind on what to do, and I had to do it without delay.

Another thirty minutes went by before I knew what room she was in, and I knocked on the door and yelled for her to open the door. What I saw was unnerving, to say the least. Jen had only a T-shirt on, and I knew she had been partying without any regard to what had happened to Didi.

Jen seemed mad that I would break up the happy time they were having, and she said, "I don't think it was a good thing for you to bust in here and start trouble for no reason."

One of the guys she was with tried to start something and I hit him in the mouth. Jen knew then that I meant business.

She looked at me I said, "You slut, do you even know what you have done?"

"What is it now, boy?" she asked.

That went all over me and I replied, "Woman, you didn't even go to your daughter in the hospital, you left her without any clothes, and I had to go to the hospital and tell her that her mom just forgot. I didn't tell her that you didn't give a fuck about her, and that you just wanted to get laid rather than be her mother. So, if you think she has a mother at all, then you are mistaken, woman!!!"

I went straight home to take care of the children and when she got there, she threw a fit and said all kinds of things about me to her boyfriend of the day. Then she went running down the road yelling all kinds of F this and F that all the way. I was on her heels telling her just what she was.

When I got back to the front yard, the boyfriend threw me down. I got up and hit him so hard it knocked him out cold. He woke up and slowly walked to the side of the house where I hit him again. I knocked him out cold again. He just lay against the fence all night before he came to. He decided he'd had enough and left.

Jen, of course, came home begging for another chance, and I knew then that if we went to Nevada she'd make a fool of herself and I would leave her there and bring the girls back home where they belonged. But, everything had to work out right for my plan to work the way I wanted it to work.

My parents found out what had happened, and asked me again if I knew what I was doing. I told them I did, but I really didn't know for sure if it would work. I told them I'd know in a couple of days.

Jen and I got our furniture and drove west. She and her cousin drove the Blazer, and I drove the U-Haul with a friend. It didn't take long before my friend asked me if I knew what I was doing. I told him that if I could tell the future I would be rich. By the way Jen and her cousin were acting, I knew in the back of my mind that it was going to be okay.

When we were in Oklahoma Jen got pulled over and got a ticket for speeding. My friend told me that he was worried about me being out west without him to help. I told him that I had to try. He warned me to watch out. I knew it wasn't going to be easy.

When we got to Nevada, my friend asked me again if I knew what I was doing. I don't think he'd seen a place as ugly as Laughlin, Nevada. He left hoping this was a good idea.

It didn't take Jen long for her true colors to come out. By the second day she had a new boyfriend. I got thrown out of the Frontier Hotel because she started some shit to get rid of me. The girls were mad about how she was treating us. I had to put up with it for a little while so things could work like I'd planned.

Well it wasn't long before things started to go the wrong way, and it was not a pretty sight. One day after I had gone to try to get a job, I got back to the house we had found. Jen had changed the locks and she said she wanted me to go! I knew then there was going to be a fight. But surprisingly, she gave in.

The girls were uneasy about the next day, much less the future. So, I stayed until Jen got back from taking Lilly to her cousin's house. But, she didn't come back. Didi was getting sick, and Catie was running a temperature. I was trying to find Jen so we could take the kids to the doctor, but no Jen.

I started getting mad. I had no diapers for Didi. I had to go down to the store and get milk and cereal and a few other things. I didn't have much money at that time. It was getting dark and I didn't even know where Lilly was. I didn't know how I was going to take care of Didi if she got sicker. I was standing in the kitchen when Catie fell into the table in the living room. As I ran to her, I tripped on my foot and slammed my hand into the couch. I knew that I had broken something, but didn't know what or how bad it was. I couldn't go see about it because the girls had to be taken care of first, and who knew when or if their mother was coming back at this point. I was in a lot of pain but I just had to suck it up because the girls were not in good shape themselves, and they always came first.

Didi was hurting badly and all I could do was hope that it didn't get worse as we all waited for Jen to return. My hand started swelling. I had to think of Catie and Didi instead of myself. I stayed up all night in pain. But, all I could think about were Didi and Catie, and wonder where Lilly was and if she was okay. As the night went on it became clear that not only were Didi and Catie not well, but my hand was in bad shape.

I was overwhelmed. I was angry. This was not a good place for Didi because of her problems with her blood and her defects that had plagued her since birth. The future of my kids did not look good.

When the morning came without any sign of help, I just cried for my girls. My plan wasn't going as I had thought. But, I was still determined to carry it out as best I could as long as I had breath in my lungs. It was the only thing that drove me at this time.

Damn! I could not believe this was happening again. I could make a good movie about our pain-filled life. Why would any parent do this to these girls? They deserved better! It was a crying shame that this was even going on.

It was getting dark again, and a whole day had passed with no word at all from Jen. Didi, thank God, was not any worse, but she wasn't any better either. Catie was still running a low temp. They both needed something other than what I had. I wasn't concerned about myself, even though I knew it would take more that just a cast to fix my hand because of the time that had gone by. My thoughts were on my girls, though, not myself. I was worried about Lilly.

Darkness came and went. It was as if another world was going on without us. It became apparent that their mother didn't care about her own children much less their welfare. I think that saying that I was angry at this point was fruitless. I just wanted the girls to get what they needed, and to hell with their mom.

It was a little over three days before Jen showed up with her family and all hell broke loose. I was, in her words, overreacting to the situation. I told her that it was obvious that she didn't care if her daughters were sick. I asked her just where the hell she was when Didi and Catie needed her.

She said that she and her new boyfriend were in Vegas enjoying their time there together. She said Lilly was at Dora's. She said she was in charge of the girls now, and that I could just go.

I started towards her, and her family stopped me. They said they would call the cops if I didn't leave. They said they'd tell the cops that I tried to hurt her. In Nevada, it was mandatory that in a domestic affair, both parties went to jail.

Then Jen told me that she had the lease changed. She put only her name on it. My name wasn't on it at all. It was a Catch 22 position that I was in. The only thing I could do was go. With my heart broken for the last time, I left. I left without my girls with me.

I went to the other side of the river and stopped at the first gas station and called my sister. I knew that my parents were in Scotland at the time. Crying, my sister sent me some money to get home to Arkansas so I could regroup. I was more determined than before to get my children out of there.

I went to the casino to get the money, and I saw Jen coming towards me. She thought she had me, but again she forgot that I was smarter than she thought.

When she got to me she said, "It doesn't have to be this way, you know."

"What way is that, Jen?"

"If you do as I say, you can see the girls any time you want."

I said, "Okay. But I have to go away for a couple of days. I will be back."

"What about your hand? You can't go without seeing a doctor about your hand," she said.

"What do you care?" I asked. But, I went to Kingman to a doctor and he said the break was too bad for me to go any longer, and I would have to have surgery.

I went back to Laughlin, and it was apparent things had to change quickly because I was in a situation unlike any I'd been in before. I would fight for my children and get them out of here. I wasn't going anywhere without them. That was not an option.

Jen's sister took me to the hospital in Kingman. Jen didn't even care what I was going through. I started having thoughts of killing her to get the children out. The whole thing drove me to fight even harder to get it right this time. The girls were all that mattered anymore to me, not my life, not anything else. Not even their mother's life mattered to me at all. I needed to get the girls home to Arkansas safely. That is where they belonged.

I remember lying on the hospital bed wondering how something so special could have gone so wrong. I didn't know the answer, but I knew there was one thing I had to do. I had to make sure that the girls had a safe life, a life without pain if at all possible.

After surgery, I came to and my hand was wrapped. The doctor said I could go if I had a ride back to Laughlin, but no one was there to take me. I asked the nurse to call, but there was no one at the house to answer the phone. I just sat there for what seemed hours while I waited for somebody to come get me, anybody at all. It didn't matter to me who. I needed to get back to the girls. Finally, Jen's sister came to take me back to the house where the girls waited for me.

Jen had gone to work, but I had to leave the house before she got back or she would call the cops being that I was not on the lease anymore. I asked Jen's sister if she knew what Jen was doing at all. She said that she loved her sister, but that she knew that the girls did not like what was going on, and she was sorry about it all.

I got some clothes and went to the Riverside Casino to talk to Jen before leaving for Arkansas. When I saw her I looked into those deep beautiful brown eyes and didn't see love anymore. I didn't see the same person I had fallen in love with. All I saw was hate; hate on top of hate. Two troubled souls who seemed to cross paths in the night instead of two people who had fallen in love, gotten married, and had three children together. Two people whose oldest child had gone through shunt revisions twelve times, heart surgeries, and blood transfusions. And two other children, who had Christenings, teacher meetings, Halloweens, and Christmases with smiles all around.

All I saw in front of me was a person that I would have no remorse for if I grabbed her and broke her neck right there. I knew then, that it was over. We would never be the same. We would never hold each other in the way of love. There were too many burned bridges, too much pain, and no more heart-filled feelings for each other. For myself, there was only pain, pain of love lost. There was no reason for it. It was truly the first and the last. The first time I would feel hatred and the last time I would look into those eyes with any feeling at all. If we had not been in a public place, I would've killed her without any thought. She was the enemy now. I don't think I had ever had so much hate for one person in my life.

She would soon find out the game was up, all the twists and turns that she had maneuvered to put me in this position would soon come to an end. And that smirk of a smile that she had on her face now would be replaced by tear-filled eyes of pain that she could never escape from. And I would have the last laugh. As she kissed me on my cheek, I felt nothing. Before, I would've felt compassion, love, and a wanting for a woman that I would never have again. And as she walked away I knew my course was set. The mission had started. And I had never failed a mission that I had set my mind to.

My hand was wrapped up from the surgery, and I just stood there as a chill went down my spine. The chill was not just cold, but filled with anger and remorse. For what I had to do would hurt all of us. But in the end, it would help the children the most. It would release them from this hell that they had been placed into.

I got my money and started the long journey back to Arkansas. Only stopping for gas, a coca-cola, and an occasional burger or candy bar, I headed home. I would not stop to rest until I was pulling into my parents' driveway in Conway.

When I got there my parents were home from Scotland and I told them what had gone on in Laughlin, and that I had but one thing on my mind and that was to get the girls home where they belonged. My dad was scared that I would be walking back into a trap, but I assured him that Jen had no idea of my plans to get the kids and come home. It would be easy. She had a firm belief that I was in no way shape or form smart enough to pull it off. She already thought that she had won. I knew my mind and what it would take to get the girls back from Nevada.

My mother was missing the girls so badly that she cried all that night thinking she would never see her grandchildren, and I knew I couldn't stop now.

"They belong here!" I said to my parents. "With all the strength I have, it will come to pass!"

I told my parents if she called that they should tell her that I was at the doctor because I was having stomach problems, and that I wouldn't be coming back for some things until I had some tests run on my stomach. Dad wondered if she would even call. I knew she would. I knew the way she thought.

Sure enough, she called. I set the trap, and she took the bait. I said goodbye to my mom and dad and started the long drive back to Laughlin. As I drove, all I could think about was getting my girls. As I got closer to them, the thought of them back in Arkansas made my drive more bearable. It took me almost 20 hours. When I got there, I slept. I hoped to see the girls for a couple of hours. I was drained. But, all I could think about was them. It consumed me.

The next day, Jen was quite friendly. It was surprising, but I wasn't fooled by the charms of a harlot.

I heard the cries of my girls saying, "Dad, Dad, oh Dad!"

I cried all the time I was with them knowing that it wouldn't be long before Jen would say I had to leave. But, she had some compassion, and she let me be with the kids for quite awhile. She told me that she had called my parents and they told her that I had to have some tests run.

I told her I may have to have some work done on my stomach.

She replied, "Well, you better go back soon to let the doctors see what is wrong with you."

I said, "Yes, but I would like to take the girls back and let them see their friends before school starts. You know they miss them."

She said, "I know they do, but I don't think that will help much knowing they won't be able to stay long." I agreed and walked away.

In a couple of days, I could tell I was getting to her. Then came the rub. We were riding in her sister's car and I said, "I think I'll get some cocaine when I go back. I could bring some back with me."

The look on her face told me that I had her right where I wanted her, and it took only one more day before she let Catie and Lilly go back with me. I tried to get her to let me take Didi, too, but she said no. I knew it would be okay, though, when she let me go ahead and take Lilly and Catie because I knew then with a little more talking she would let Didi go, but later.

So I started the long trip back to Arkansas. It was the Fourth of July weekend and traffic was pretty bad to say the least. I knew Lilly and Catie were happy to be coming back home. I knew my mom and dad would be very happy to see the girls. I was just overly tired to begin with and this trip took all I had to make it back without stopping.

When we got to Conway, I stopped at a gas station and tried to call my parents. No one answered. I waited a little while longer and called again. This time my dad answered the phone and I said hi and asked him to put mom on the phone. When she got on the phone I asked her if she'd like to see her grandkids.

She started crying and said, "What do you think, A.J.?"

I told her to open her door in a few minutes.

I drove the short drive out to their house on the lake. When we got there my parents were in tears. The girls ran out of the car yelling, "Nana, Nana, oh, Nana!"

The girls loved my mom and dad and were glad to be home. I got out of the car so tired that I fell into my dad's arms and told him I had to get some sleep.

I awoke to fresh coffee filling the air as it always did when I was at my parents' house, and I walked in to see the joy on the girls' faces. I knew then it was the right place for them. It was home, and home was where they belonged.

Then, Mom asked about Didi, and I told her that Jen would not let her come. I could see the anger in her face. I gave her a hug and told her next time.

I thought the girls knew I was planning on taking them back, but to their credit they did not say so. It was a good trip for them because they got to see their friends, and they also got to be with my parents. This wasn't about me and their mother, it was about their happiness, and that meant being home which was here, not in Nevada.

After a few days I got to thinking about how to make Jen think that I was going to bring some shit back and also make it seem to the kids that I wasn't thinking about taking them back home after all. So, I went to a bar and got with some dumb ass girls that would think about going with me to gamble in Nevada and not about what was really going on. This part was a lie, but it would serve its purpose.

We said goodbye to my mom and dad and I told the girls that I was going to have some other girls go back with us. Lilly was not dumb, and she didn't like the idea, but she didn't say anything. Catie was a little too young to know the difference, which also made it more believeable that all I was doing was the same old thing. I got just enough stuff to get the girls high and get me out to Laughlin, and away we went.

Lilly wasn't happy about that, but I knew that if it worked that she would know it was for the best. So as we made our way back it was clear to me that Jen did not know what was coming, or who for that matter. As we got closer I had to fake as if I was high to make it real.

It was about two in the morning when we got there. I took my girls to where they were staying, and their mom was not there. I told the person who was there that I was going to go and get a room, and that I would see the girls in the morning. I kissed the girls and told them that I loved them.

Then the phone rang. It was Jen's brother asking if I brought some "stuff". He got mad as hell and was throwing a fit on the phone because I told him that I did all the shit on the way. I took the two girls who were with me to the Edgewater Hotel and Casino and got a room. I was dog tired, and the girls were real excited about going gambling. They were putting make up on when I was in the shower.

I got out of the shower, and I was putting my pants on when Jen and Sheri came busting in and started hitting the girls and cussing like sailors. Evidently Jen knew someone at the registration desk and found out what room I was in and got the key.

I tossed Sheri up against the wall, and told Jen to calm down. As I was trying to hold her, Sheri came at me again, and Jen tried taking the pins out of my thumb at the same time. With my thumb bleeding, I started to lose my temper. The girls were down the hall by this time, and I was still wrestling with Jen and her sister. Getting thrown against the wall one more time was enough for Sheri. She realized I wasn't the person she needed to be messing with. Jen on the other hand, was still trying to take the pins, which were exposed, out of my thumb. I flipped her over the bed, held her arms down, and sat on her chest. I was yelling at her to stop.

The next thing I knew, a Clark County Sheriff had a gun at the back of my head. They handcuffed Jen and me, and took us down to a secured location. Jen was yelling, and cussing the whole way down. She was telling them that I was the devil, and that I was threatening the lives of her and her children. They kept Jen handcuffed, but saw the blood dripping from the end of my thumb. They asked me if I would behave if they take the handcuffs off. I told them I would.

Jen was yelling, "He has ounces of cocaine in the Blazer!"

Since the officers already had my keys, I told them that that wasn't true, that I brought two of our children from Arkansas, dropped them off at their house, and had no idea what the hell she was talking about. I also told the officers where I was parked, and that they were more than welcome to search my Blazer. Two of the officers went to do that very thing, and the other two had to stay and listen to Jen tell them how bad of a dad and husband I was. She couldn't wait for them to find the cocaine and lock me up in prison so I would never see my children again.

As she glared at me, with nothing but hate, I glared back, knowing I had her right where I wanted her. I kept shaking my head while she was cursing me, telling the officers that I had no idea what she was talking about, that I had full custody of the girls for a reason, and how she had lost her mind.

It was at that time, that the other two officers came back in and said, "Ma'am, there is nothing in the Blazer, nothing in the room, and no reason to suspect he had anything in the first place. And since you are showing your ass and it's obvious, sir, that your thumb is broken and that your ex-wife tried to do something to it during the fight, we will let you go. But, Ma'am, we are taking you to Clark County Jail in Las Vegas where you will have twelve hours to cool down and to think about what you have just done."

I had a smirk smile on my face, and she was yelling, "He's lying!"

They escorted Jen, kicking and screaming, and I went back to the room.

The girls who came with me had the bags already packed and said, "We're driving back to Arkasas and you're coming with us."

I was in a lot of pain. I had a couple of pain pills with me. I took them and lay down in the back. The next thing I knew, I was waking up in Arkansas. I then drove to my parents' house. My dad and mom had already heard from Jen, and they gave her a piece of their mind. They asked me what happened. I told them, and then I went to sleep.

When I woke up they gave me a thousand dollars and said go get our grandchildren and come home. I drove straight through, only stopping for gas. I didn't even eat. When I got to where Jen and the kids were staying, Jen's step-mother was there. She took me out to where she had the girls. Didi was by a bunch of rocks by the river in her wheel chair. Lilly and Catie were burned from the hot sun, being that it was about 130 degrees, and Didi was sweating to death with a baseball cap and fully clothed.

I looked at Jen and said, "If you thought I would bring a bunch of cocaine out here and get set up you're crazy. I have to go see a doctor about my thumb and about my stomach. There are three weeks before schools starts, let me take the girls back with me so I can see if there's something wrong with me and then I'll bring them back."

I knew Jen wanted to get drunk and screw somebody, and she was working. I knew the girls were in her way. Sure enough, she said yes without any hesitation.

I quickly told the girls to get in the Blazer. I wheeled Didi behind the two younger girls. Even though it was approaching night fall, I grabbed a couple of pillows, a couple of blankets, and a couple of outfits for them all and took off.

As I pulled over at a Shell station going up the hill towards Kingman right outside of Bullhead City, Arizona, the girls were almost asleep in the car. I smiled as I was filling up the tank with gas and thought, "Hook, line, and sinker!"

The four of us headed home for the final time. When we got to Conway I was so tired I fell into my mother's arms. The girls, especially Didi, were so happy that they started to cry. I was just glad that we made it back home, and I hopefully did not ever have to make that trip again. The kids were where they belonged. I thought that this day would never come, but I had hoped that it would, and it did.

The next day I made sure that the girls were enrolled in school. Then I went to the lawyer's office and made sure he made it impossible for Jen to ever have a way to get custody of the girls. Ever!

My dad and I went to the house where Jen and I had raised the girls. We got some furniture and beds. I wanted the girls to have a place they could finally call home. Then we went back to my parents' house and kissed the girls and went to sleep.

I woke up happy and rested. The girls were anxious to see their friends. I loaded them up and took them to the house.

As we walked into our house I said, "This is your home. I think it would be better for you to stay here, so I am not taking you back to Nevada. This is where you belong. Your friends are here and you will live your lives in peace here. What do you think?"

Didi said, "Dad, we want to be with you. We love you."

I gave them a hug and kiss. I told them that I would have to call their mother and let her know. I told them she would want to talk to them. They said they'd let her know this is where they wanted to be. Didi called her mother and told her they lived with me now, and if she wanted to see them, she would just have to come to Conway. I thought it was the bravest thing that a young girl could do. I was proud of all of them. They told me they were proud of me. I will never forget that as long as I live.

Jen, on the other hand, was crying when she called back. She said she knew what I was going to do. I asked her why she didn't try to stop me. She had no answer for that. I knew she was trying to play on my heart with that comment.

I said, "If you were so concerned with the girls, why didn't you take care of them instead of trying to get my ass in jail?"

She didn't have an answer for that either.

I continued, "They belong to me and I have custody of them. If you ever want to see them again, you'll have to come here. Okay! Woman, do you think you could ever outthink me? Do you still think that I am, how did you put it? Oh, yeah, predictable? Wasn't that it?!!"

She started to cry, and I said, "Don't, Girl! I am not the boy that you always thought I was. I am a man, Woman! And don't you ever think I am not!"

That was the last time I heard from her for four years. That hurt the girls a lot. I do not think they ever forgave their mother for that.

CHAPTER 17
Life On Life's Terms

    The girls started school with a smile knowing that they were home to stay. As it turned out, I started taking them to the NA meetings in North Little Rock with me. There I met people who became my friends. I finally felt like I belonged.

    Recovery became part of all our lives for the next few months. I had friends I could and would talk to about all the things I couldn't talk about to anybody, much less my parents. I felt good. These people made me feel like I could do this if I really wanted to. They all fell in love with the girls, and like everywhere she went Didi was the pet of the place, and life was good, at least for awhile.

    These people were the program to me, and most of them are still here today. I will never forget what they put into my head, and that was recovery, and the feeling of peace for us all. Boy did we have some fun, too. We were always together at the Starlite Café, and the movies, and at campouts. We seemed to have cookouts and parties all the time. We were a close group and we got along pretty good.

    I don't know if they knew how much they meant to the girls and me, and I will always look back and think of them as the best group of people that I will ever be a part of, in and out of recovery. They will always be in my heart, and the idea that was put into place then will always be what I remember the most. The togetherness in that group is still in me today.

It wasn't always like that. I remember when I started going it was difficult for me to do the things that they asked me to do because I was not openminded at all. To all people who tried recovery, the mere thought of change got them all stuck on stupid, and I was no different than anybody else.

My sponsor told me if I wanted to change, I would have to be willing to think in a different way. But, my thinking always got in the way, and that got me in trouble. Even though I got a lot out of the group it was my thoughts that always drove me to go back out and do what I always did, and that was to get high. Trouble followed me all the way. I always got into more trouble. I loved the people in the meeting but I always got in my own way of my recovery. In fact it always got me in places that I never thought I would be.

I remember saying that I would never do crack, and I did. I remember that I said that I would not ever go back to doing the needle, but I did that, too. It was my thoughts that always got in the way of my recovery and to a bottom that I never thought I would get to.

I had year or so clean, and I just gave it away for the fuck of it. It was frustrating to say the least, and I thought that if I just made up my mind I could get clean. But that was my problem. I always turned to myself instead of turning to the group to help me. I could not see that I was the problem. I would say it was the group, but in reality it was the disease of addiction. Most of us could not see that for what it really was. I had to learn that I wasn't a bad person. It was my disease that was the problem. The more I fought it, the worse it got.

Didi was going through a rough time with her transfusions. For three or four months, she would get a transfusion, and then it would be only a couple of weeks before she would need another one. It was a bad time for everyone, and I surely wasn't helping by getting high. But that is the nature of the beast. I just kept doing the same thing expecting different results. That is insanity.

I had a friend who had a problem with the Feds and one day the Feds came to my house questioning me. I was doing a lot of cocaine at the time. I just wanted them to leave, so I said something to them.

Being high, I really didn't even realize what I said. It must have been what they wanted to hear, though, because we all got busted.

I didn't realize at the time that it was Didi and the girls who would be affected the most by my actions. When I was in my active addiction I just didn't think about a lot of things. I just thought about how and where to get more of what I wanted. I didn't think about what mattered the most. Everything was about me. I had a sick feeling that all this was my fault.

I felt guilt about everything. It must have been my fault my marriage fell apart. If I were a better father to Didi she wouldn't be having these problems. All this thinking fueled my addiction. That's how my addiction got to me. It was the guilt, remorse, anger, and shame. Instead of letting go and letting God, I just thought about how it was all my fault.

I remember my sponsor wanted me to do a fourth step. He wanted me to write something down. I thought I was different than everyone else and I put it on micro cassette. I was proud of it. When I took it to him, in front of the group, he threw it on the ground and stomped on it and it broke. I was mad as hell at him. He told me to write it down! I just went off. I had tried to take a shortcut. I wouldn't listen to anybody and I surely would not do what was right when it came to me. Hell! That was unthinkable to me at that time in my recovery and addiction. Little did I know I was about to find out just how my actions would affect the rest of my life and the lives of my girls.

I was at home when the police came again to talk to me about that so called friend of mine, and yes I was high at the time so I told them the same thing. It would be something that I would regret forever. It was around this time that Didi had her worst problem with her blood, and when I got home one day she was almost blue. That was a sign that her blood level was bad low. I called the doctor as I always did and took her to the hospital. My parents helped me with Lilly and Catie. As I left for the hospital I could tell she was not felling good at all. I was worried more this time because of how blue she was. It reminded me of the time she had her surgery on her heart. I was worried.

She looked up at me and said, "Dad, I don't want to die."

Then I really started to get worried that I might not get to the hospital in time. This was the first time she had ever said that. It was the first time I had considered the possibility of her going. I was scared to death.

When we got to the hospital, the doctors knew how bad it was. They started the transfusion process. This was the best hospital, but it still crossed my mind that this could be the time I had feared all her life. It was about four in the morning and I was very high. I just couldn't seem to get that thought that I might lose her out of my mind.

As she cried, it got worse. Would she make it, or not? The feeling of not knowing if I would be in any shape to handle God's will worried me, too. Would I just crumble under the stress of the moment? I didn't know, and I would not know for awhile. It was that bad. I called my parents to tell them how bad it was this time. That didn't seem to ease my pain or my inadequate feeling. Again, I was thinking more about me. It was always more about me. It was driving me insane.

As always, Didi was fighting. She just lay there and said, "Dad, do not go anywhere. Please, Dad, don't go anywhere!"

"I won't, Didi," I told her. By this time it was about 9 or 10 o'clock in the morning and the doctors still didn't know if we had gotten there in time. Then heartbreak came. The attorney for the feds called and said I had to be at the federal building to testify for them in the case against that so called friend of mine. The doctors faxed a letter to them telling them the state my daughter was in. To my surprise, the attorney said I had to be at the federal building anyway. And there lay Didi crying and still begging me not to leave.

It wasn't long before a U.S. Marshall called me and told me I had to testify. I told him to talk to the doctor. The doctor told him about Didi's condition. He said he'd call me back.

A few minutes later, the call that changed my life came. The U.S. Marshall said, "If you are not here in fifteen minutes, we will come and arrest you and make sure you never see your daughter again!"

I could not believe what I was just told. It was as if I was already in hell and had no way out. Didi could see that I was crying. I did not know what to do. She started to cry again.

She said, "Dad, please!"

"Baby, I have to go for a minute. You just hold on for me. Okay?"

I couldn't believe it but I had to leave my beautiful daughter not knowing if she would be alive when I got back or not. I was raging! The closer I got to the federal building, the more rage I felt.

I got there and my so called friend said he wasn't going to lose any sleep over this, and he told me not to be angry.

"Don't be angry!!! You son-of-a-bitch! Your daughter is not fighting for her life right now, so you can kiss my ass!!"

Then I heard an attorney telling someone that if I didn't say what they wanted, he would make sure they got me on tax evasion or something else.

That made me mad, so I shouted, "I know who you are and where you live, Boy!!!"

Then I got up to call the hospital to ask about Didi. They told me there was no change. I went back to wait to testify to the grand jury. Another hour went by. They had told me it would only take about 50 minutes or so, and it was already over three hours. I was past the point of rage.

Finally, they called me. I got on the stand to testify, and I told them what they wanted to hear. I wanted to get back to Didi as quickly as possible.

Thank God, by the time I got back to the hospital, Didi had stabilized. I kissed her and told her I loved her.

She said, "Dad, I held on for you!"

I cried like a baby. The doctor told me it was touch and go for awhile, but that she'd be okay. Didi would have to stay for a day or so, but then she would be fine.

Didi said, "Dad, I'm okay. You go now and see about Lilly and Catie."

I could not believe the courage of this little girl, my daughter.

I went as fast as I could to a pay phone to call my parents and tell them how Didi was doing and I told them to tell Lilly and Catie. Then I called my so called friend that I testified against. I told him to bring his wife and meet me at my house. I told him they better be there. He said they would.

I drove to my house thinking about this day. It was unbelievable. I met the friend, and told them what had been going on. I told them I had to leave my baby to testify. They couldn't believe it. They said they would have done the same thing.

That's when I shouted, "You do not have to worry about me in court. Didi was worth more than you. I will tell the truth in court!"

They gave me what I asked for; more cocaine. Boy, what a trade off; my honor for some shit. Now that is addiction. I traded my soul for something that didn't even get me high anymore.

That's when I decided to go back to meetings again with the kids. It was funny watching how everyone loved the girls, and how they acted at the meetings. Catie was the most unruly kid there. I remember how they all loved Didi. I think Lilly was still a little intimidated by the people at the meeting. She just wanted to be at home instead of there anyway, so I guess looking back it was funny how differently the kids reacted to it all.

After meetings, we'd go to Starlite Café. That in itself was the funniest thing because that was the highlight of their whole trip to the meetings. They knew we'd go there after every meeting. How they loved that place!

I look back at that time of my life and I know that for a while my children and I were happy in the short time that we had together. But, it would not take long for my addiction to get in the way as it always did. I was longing for something, and as before I thought that a relationship was what I needed. As always, it was not the thing I needed. It was my downfall.

I was at home one day when the Feds came. The local police found me home first. I was mad when they asked who the nigger was, and so were the kids. You see Margie, my housekeeper and my babysitter, was a good woman. As it always was for me and all the people who worked for me, I did not see color. I saw a person that was trying as we all were to do what we could for each other in a way that we could be proud of. I was ashamed when they said that about a woman who was as great a lady as there was in this world. That just showed the divide that this country still had, and how the powers that be can destroy a life if you let them. The police came into my home and disrespected my house, my children, and the lady that watched them.

I asked the police why they were at my house. They just said that I was a criminal and I was to be put in jail for lying to the grand jury. You see I kept my word to that so called friend of mine and when court came, I not only tore up the attorney in charge of the case, but I also told the truth.

I told them, "No, I wasn't the money man, and I did not help the guy avoid paying taxes. I was just an addict who was mad because they put their case in front of my daughter. To me, that was it in a nutshell."

I had to have my sister get the money to get me out on bond. My parents were in Scotland, and they were not in the position to help. I was convicted by the same judge that pardoned the president for the same thing, but that is how the powerful people do the things they do, and get away with it. Life on life's terms. It will fuck up one's idea of what we think is the right thing to do.

The fact was that I lied and I had to pay for it. Facing that was a hard thing for me to do seeing that what I did was the right thing in my mind, but in the reality of life it was still lying. I had to pay a price for that, and that price was my freedom. In life there are always things that you pay for and things that you do not pay for. I had a lot to pay for and I could not hide from it all. Like most things in my past it was catching up to me, and like most people I did not like it. But, what does not kill you makes you strong, right? I was not strong in my eyes. I was weak, and to surrender was not seen as the strong thing to do. In reality surrender became my greatest strength, but I had to wait to realize that. I was not ready. I had to fail some more of life on life's terms before I could surrender to God's will for me.

CHAPTER 18
Time to Pay!

I thought that I was so cool at telling my girls how to do a lot of things, but I did not know shit about the things they needed the most. They needed a father who would teach them how to deal with life on life's terms. I needed to teach them how to say no to what got their father in trouble his whole life. When you do what you have always done then you get what you always got. And when you think the way you have always thought then you get what life will give you. I wasn't prepared for what was next. I got a five year sentence for perjury in the case when I lied to the grand jury. I had to do time for that crime. Then, after I failed a drug test they put me in jail. My girlfriend at the time kept in touch with the girls. They were staying with my parents. My dad wouldn't even let me get near to his house or the business. I had taken checks to Wal-Mart and cashed them for thousands of dollars. Then I would take that to the drug man and do drugs all night. My life was unmanageable. That was the case for most of my life. I just could not see it because I thought that someone would bail me out like they always had. This time though, my parents were fed up with me, and their answer was no.

I was in jail when Didi got sick. My parents did not tell me. The county jail was not where I wanted to be the day of the Super Bowl either. But there I was.

One day in jail, my name was called to go to court. I told them I had already been sentenced. When they made me go on to court, I stood in front of the judge.

My parents showed up, and the judge said, "Time served and probation!"

I told my dad to get me out of there before the judge changed his mind. He drove me to his house where I was ordered to stay. All I could think about was seeing my kids. I also couldn't wait to go back to the meetings before I got in trouble again.

Things seemed to work out for a while, but I was doing things for the wrong reasons and not for myself. I also was thinking about Sydney. I wondered if I would ever see her again. I wondered if her mother would ever let me see her. It was a time for reflection on the things that I regretted the most. At the top of that list was Sydney. I wondered if my girls would ever have a father that they could or would be proud of. I blamed myself for everything, but I still did not know enough about the disease.

I had to think I was a good person. I had to work an honest third step to get things close to where I wanted them to be. I wanted to be a good father and husband, but I was far from that. I had to fight the demon that ruled my thinking. That demon was addiction. The thoughts that came with loneliness were mine to bear.

I was in the middle of another relapse when the door slammed on the cold reality of life on life's terms. I did not know just how bad things could get, but I was on the verge of finding out, and I surely was not prepared for it at all. I gave a bad drug test and the feds put me into a halfway house in Little Rock. I was not pleased by that at all, but knowing that I was using was a fact that I had to pay for.

Here I was again going through the motions but not doing a thing about it. I was going to meetings, but I was not working the steps that I needed to work. It was clear to everyone else that I could not, and would not work an honest third step. But it wasn't clear to me! The simple thing to do was listen, but being in active addiction, I wouldn't listen at all. Even when seven or eight people were telling me that I needed to do something, I still wouldn't listen. I was not working the program at all.

The program was too simple for me to get. I made it harder than it really was. A program that I had been involved with for so long should be simple. But, I was mentally incapable of getting it. Was I trying too hard? My thinking was the problem, not the steps or anything else. I was the only thing that was getting in the way. I would not let go and let God. I did not know how to do that. I wanted some control back. I did not realize that I had never had any to begin with.

During this time, I was still confused about how to do the right thing when it came to living the program. I needed to do right by the kids. Like always, I got into another relationship with a girl from the program. It was good for awhile. Jen was calling and talking to me and the girls. I wasn't satisfied with the relationship I was in. I guess as always it was more me than it was her, but the girls did not like her anyway. It turned out that she was hitting the girls, and I did not like that. The girls did not really like anyone I was with. I was all they had, and they didn't want to share me.

I started using again. It wasn't a good thing at all. I failed a drug test, so the feds put me in the halfway house again. I had to straighten up or I would be in deep shit. I started going back to the meetings and trying to do the right thing, but it would not last. I had to be honest with myself or it would never work. I just couldn't figure out what I was doing wrong. I surrounded myself with the wrong people all the time. When I was in the meetings I would always be attracted to the new people. When I was high, I would trust people who couldn't be trusted at all. Insane thinking wasn't getting me anywhere.

I remember being told if I really meant what I said then I would work some steps and figure out my thinking was not getting me anywhere but high like always. I just was not ready for it, and anybody can tell you that if a person is not ready to get clean and work the program to the best of their ability then they just need to go out and get some more misery. Then maybe, just maybe they will make it back. Most of the time they don't, but every once in a while it works out that a person gets enough and they come back in and are willing to do the right thing. The right thing is to work the steps the program has to offer. When they do that, they see the mistakes of their thinking. People just aren't willing to change. That is the main problem. The program is a "we" program, not an "I" program.

Finally, things seemed to be going well, and I was beginning to see how my thinking was what I had to change. But the shame, blame with no gain was still in the back of my mind. My disease was working all the time, and my recovery was spotted at best. It was new to me even though I had been involved in the family of NA for a long time. I was just not willing enough to fight with the strangers all around me. My guilt and the feeling of blame kept me from fighting. My mind was working overtime against me, and I gave into that thinking once again.

I set up what would be the most damaging thing that I would ever go through in my life. It was just around the corner, too. It was the thing that would change my life forever. In many ways all of us, the girls and my parents, would never be the same.

A beautiful day became the nightmare's last ditch effort to try to kill my sense of worth. It almost worked, too. If it wasn't for the program, the things I thought I hadn't listened to but really did, I don't think I would have survived it. The nightmare that I had been living was just about to make me experience the worst that life has to offer. And, instead of becoming the thing that would be my undoing, it became the way for me to be willing to change at last.

It all started with a cold. I thought I could just take an antihistamine and some drugs to get high on. Thus, I failed another drug test. I tried to tell the authorities it was the over-the-counter medicine that caused me to fail the test.

Then there was the girl. I broke up with her because I didn't want her to go down with me. I drove away all the people who cared about me the most. What I really wanted to do was to die. I didn't want to recover. This game of hit and miss would come to a sudden and horrible end. I couldn't handle anything at that time in my life. I thought of the saying "others must die for some to live".

It was May 1997. I was called into the office of the halfway house, and the people there told me that I had turned in a dirty pee test and I would be going for my hearing to find out if the feds would put me in prison or not. Well, I told them I was leaving and they could all go to hell. That's what an addict says when they don't get their way. They blame everyone else but themselves.

I headed out and ran into a friend. I decided to drive her to see her boyfriend in the southern part of Missouri. It took all night to get there and back. On the way, I remembered telling my father the week before that I had set up a power of attorney for my ownership of the business and all my things I still had. I also had told him that I knew I had not been the son he wanted, but I wanted him to take care of the girls. As I was driving back home, all those thoughts were in my head again for some reason. I realized that if I was going to make it, I had to do it for myself.

    Well, I wasn't watching my speed, and I got a speeding ticket as I entered Little Rock. I decided to go to a friend's house in town. I knew she had some shit there, but I didn't do any. I had enough in me already. I called a hooker, though, to do me so I could sleep. I needed sleep before taking the girls for our drive the next day.

    I slept for awhile, and then I drove to Conway to get the girls. Lilly was in Florida on a band trip, so it was just Didi and Catie who would be with me. My parents wanted me to stay and drive around in Conway, but the girls wanted to go to the Starlite. We decided to go to Little Rock to the Starlite, and then after we ate there, we would make up our minds about where we'd drive.

    As we drove off in my new 3000 GT, I thought we'd have a fun day. I didn't, in my wildest dreams, know it would be the day to end all days for me. As we drove south, I decided to stop at my friend's place in Jacksonville. I knew she had a hit at her place. I could get it if I wanted it. It was that thought in my mind that would be my undoing in the end.

    As an addict, I was driven by a terrible thought pattern even though I was having a good day. I was self-centered and always had been. That was the core of my disease. We were having a great day, but still, being an addict, that didn't matter. It never mattered whether I was having a good day or a great day. I was always consumed with the thought of what I wanted.

    After we ate, I picked up a friend and we all went to a tattoo shop. The girls sat in the car and I went in to see about getting a new tattoo. My friend sat in the car with the girls. Everything seemed to be going just perfect and all of us were having loads of fun.

    I got my tattoo and we took off. It was a beautiful day. There was a festival going on so Little Rock was packed with traffic. I decided to go to Jacksonville to top off the day with what I wanted most of all. Getting a hit was what I wanted to do.

    Any other father would never have wanted that to top off a wonderful day. But, I thought it would make everything just right. I thought that would just make the day perfect when in fact, nothing could have made the day better than it already was. I couldn't have asked for a better day.

I remember Didi and Catie were arguing about who was going to be in the front seat with me, but Catie was too small, and Didi really needed to be in the back with her sister. But I gave in and let Didi sit up front with me. As we pulled away from the shop, I headed to Jacksonville.

The traffic was bad and it took us a little while to get on the highway. I looked over at Didi and she had a smile on her face. Traffic got heavier because of a double tractor-trailer accident on the south side. I remember looking over and noticing the sun beaming brightly through the clouds and everything seemed perfect.

Suddenly, without warning, all the cars in front of me started slamming on their brakes and there was no way of avoiding the tragedy that was about to happen.

I still remember the green Stelth in front of me bearing the license plate TOYTOY. I was only doing about 35 miles an hour, but it still caused a domino effect. For some reason I did not put my arm out to protect Didi, as I usually did. My air bag opened so hard that I was in a daze. Catie was seated behind me screaming, and smoke was coming from the hood.

I looked over and I was shocked to see Didi lying motionless in the front seat next to me. I called her name, but there was no answer. I reached over. Her eyes were half shut and her body lay limp in the seat. I yelled her name louder, but still received no response.

Catie yelled loudly in my ear, "Dad, help her, help her!"

I held Didi close, but still got no response. Her bottom lip was split down to her chin, yet there was no blood to be seen.

I was screaming, "Lord! No! Lord! No!" People were running up to the car to see if they could help. One person reached in for Didi to see if they could help.

I screamed, "No, No! I couldn't bear to let her go. I screamed again. My friend in the back seat began to yell for someone to call an ambulance. All I could do was continue to cry and still scream. Catie was still screaming in my ear, too. I began crying even harder. I had always told Didi that I would save her from the boogie man, yet I felt as if I had become the boogie man. You see her air bag did not open until her frail head hit the dashboard, and once it did, it virtually ripped her apart. I was shaking and probably in shock at this point. It seemed that I could feel her life leaving her body, and I continued to scream, "No Lord, no Lord!"

Catie continued to scream, "Save her Dad!"

I didn't want to believe it, but she was gone.

I could not understand how this could happen. I sat there with guilt and shame running through my body. The only reason why I was even on that road was to go get a hit.

Catie began yelling, "Didi, wake up!"

But Didi did not respond. I called her name. I held her tight, as tears rolled down my cheeks.

I heard an ambulance getting closer, the siren echoing louder the closer it got to us. When the EMTs got to the car, they wanted to take Didi. I asked them if they were from Children's Hospital. They were not, so I told them she needed an ambulance from Children's because she was handicapped. I refused to give her to them. They told me that would take longer, and they wanted to attend to her immediately. I insisted that she be taken to Children's.

I told my friend to get out and take Catie with him, but Catie wouldn't leave her sister. Catie was frozen in the car still screaming. I couldn't let go. I could not help her. All I could do was hold Didi in my arms and cry, rocking back and forth as other people crowded around to help. I thanked them, but informed them that only God could help her now.

By this time my head was about to break in half. I was having pain from my head to my chest and my legs would not move. I still begged my baby to wake up. I kept asking the Lord not to let this happen. I begged Him to take me, not her.

It took another 30 minutes or so before the next ambulance arrived. When the EMTs arrived from Children's, they had to pry my arms from around Didi. As they came to the car, I recognized a couple of the EMTs and they recognized us. They also began to cry. As many times as we had been with Didi to Children's, we were like family. A couple of them looked at me and they were shaking their head from side to side as if confirming what I already knew in my heart.

Didi was gone. She had a faint pulse as they pried her out of the car and took her to the ambulance to work on her. I began holding Catie and looked out into the sunset. It was as if the universe was saying farewell to such a beautiful, beautiful baby. I will never forget that beautiful sunset to this day.

Catie walked over and was standing next to a state trooper and I began to yell, "Come on baby, we've got to go."

The EMT informed me that Catie could not go in the ambulance. My heart began to sink. They said there was not enough room. Catie's frightened little face stared back at me. She couldn't understand why she couldn't go.

I said, "Baby, look at me. You have to stay with the policeman."

I told him to take care of my little girl. He grabbed her up and she rode with him to the hospital.

I told the ambulance driver, "Hurry, damnit, lets go!" I was begging Didi to hold on as the ambulance drove to the hospital. Out the back window I could see Catie getting farther and farther away.

Shock, terror, and uncertainty filled my mind as we drove to the hospital. When we got there, they began working on Didi's half clothed body. I'll never forget the image of her as they rolled her into the ER.

The RN grabbed my arm and told me to let them work on Didi. Three nurses said there was nothing I could do as they pulled me away and led me to a private waiting room. I knew from that waiting room, what was going on. A chill went down my spine as I looked around at the picture frames on the walls filled with Bible quotes. I sat and rocked back and forth with the blood still on my shirt. I did not know what to do.

After approximately 20 minutes, the doctor from hematology along with another doctor came in. I knew what they were going to say.

I said to them, "She's gone, isn't she?"

They both shook their head yes and I began crying. I could not stop. I could not believe all of this was happening. After 17 years of her life being spared for it all to end like this, and I could not save her. About that time the door opened slowly.

Catie came running into my arms and asked, "How is my sister?"

I had to tell her, "She is gone, baby. She is gone."

Catie began to scream, "No! No! Why did God do this to her?"

We held each other tight and I told her it wasn't God's doing. It was mine.

The ER doctor came in to ask if we wanted to donate any of her organs. Catie looked at him as if she couldn't believe he asked that. I told him that we would donate her organs. I felt as if they were just asking me to prepare her for surgery.

I reached for the phone to call my parents. I could not get an outside line so I told Catie to stay in the waiting room so I could go call my parents. She didn't want to stay so I asked one of the doctors to stay with her. She screamed as I walked away. All the doctors and nurses paused and looked at me as if they were at a loss for words. They all knew our family.

I went to the pay phone to call my parents collect but there was no answer. I was shocked and still crying. When I walked back, the doors to Didi's room were shut. I was not sure if I could see her lifeless body lying there. The realization came to me that I would have to see her like that. I started having severe chest pains as I walked back into the waiting room where Catie was. She told me not to leave her again. About 15 minutes later I grabbed her hand and we walked through the ER, with everyone looking at us. We walked to the pay phone. I was holding Catie with my right hand as I dialed the phone, but once again there was no answer. This time Catie held me tightly around the waist as we walked back to the waiting room.

We were both in shock as we sat down. A few minutes later the waiting room door opened slowly and a state trooper appeared. He stated that it was customary, in an accident involving the death of a minor, that the driver take a blood test. He informed Catie that she would have to stay in the waiting room alone. The doctor hugged me with tears in his eyes, and he told me he was sorry but had others he must attend to. I went across the hall to another room, and the officer rudely said that he knew my background.

I replied, "Who gives a damn!" He then asked if I was on any drugs. I told him I had a cold and had taken Comtrex. He told me Comtrex would come back as an amphetamine on a blood screen.

I rolled back my sleeve, put my arm on the table and said, "I just lost my daughter in a car wreck. Do you think I give a damn? You can't do anything to me now." Tears rolled down my face. He drew the blood and said that he would have to report it.

I walked back to Catie in the waiting room, grabbed her by the hand, and went back to the pay phone. There was still no answer. We walked over to my friend. He hugged my neck and said he could not understand what was keeping me going, and he could not understand how I appeared so calm. I shook my head and thought if only he knew what was going on in my heart and mind....I just lost the most precious thing in my life and I was not calm inside.

It was not five minutes later that the doctor informed me I could see Didi. I was scared to death as the thoughts raced through my head. How can I do this? Can I handle this? How will Catie handle it? I told my friend to wait. I grabbed Catie gently by the hand and we walked to the room where Didi lay.

All the nurses watched us. They were crying as were the doctors. I took one deep breath as I walked into the room and saw the horrible sight of Didi lying there with ice over her eyes, an ice pack on her chest, and a trach tube hanging out of her throat. I grabbed her ice cold hand as I closed my eyes and cried. Catie was crying, and she fell to her knees almost in a panic state while holding my hand.

She cried, "That is not my sister. That can't be my sister. That is not Didi." I could not say anything in response. She was a precious young child, and she was being subjected to this horror. My heart broke even more. I felt as if I had let the whole world down. I could only kiss Didi on her hand. I was so scared that I could not even kiss her on the cheek. Catie got up slowly and kissed Didi on the cheek and walked out of the room.

Outside two nurses that had known Didi all her life were crying and holding each other while looking at me as if I were a criminal. I felt like one as well. I began to hate God at that moment. It turned out that it was not God I hated. I hated myself for what I had done to my precious daughter.

I went back to my friend and he grabbed me and told me that we needed to go outside. I hesitated at first and then finally agreed as I took Catie by the hand. We were going to try to reach my parents on the phone on the way out. I tried the phone one more time, but there was still no answer. At this point the panic set in.

The only person I could think to call was my uncle. His wife answered the phone and I told her what happened. I told her I couldn't reach my parents, and she said she'd come and get Catie and me. I told her to please hurry. She began to cry.

I started back to the waiting room and my friend grabbed me and told me that we needed to go outside that I probably needed a cigarette. We all walked outside, and all I could think about was good times, bad times, surgery after surgery and other thoughts circling my mind. I was in a state of confusion.

All of the sudden, sitting on the curb, I looked up to my friend and asked him to go find me a piece of paper and a pen. He asked why. I told him I needed a pen and paper. Catie looked at me and I told her that there was something I had to write about her sister. I had not written in about 20 years but I had some thoughts stuck in my head. For the first time I had thoughts about my life with my daughter that I had to get on paper.

Didi,
You came into our lives, so small, fragile, full of strength. I smile at memories of your smile. Hopeless of a future with you. Constantly troubled parents, just loaded with wonders as you proved doctors wrong. As you willingly went on. Hope to the hopeless, strength to the weak you gave. Values you instilled are in place because of your courage. Good times and bad, your smile and laughter made the tears flow away. Even as your mother's like character came through, and finger pointing messages rang true, your sisters stood up for you. You'll never know how your life made the foundation for us to follow an easier one. Today your pain is over, no longer shall you cry, know that you can fly. You're the wind beneath my wings, Strength you gave us, laughter you showed us, your memories inspire us. Joy instills us because we know that today no chair will hold you, no pain will trouble you, as you walk with Jesus today. Fly my baby, fly. We say goodbye, until we walk together with you….Your Father

My friend and his girlfriend began crying when they read this. They stated there would never be another like me, to which I replied, "I hope not."

It did not matter that my air bag opened and hers didn't; it no longer mattered that it was an unavoidable wreck. The only thing I could think of was after a beautiful day with my children, we were on that road so I could get high. I felt ashamed, angry, resentful and mad at God, real mad at God!

My uncle pulled up at the ER as I hugged my friend and his girlfriend and said goodbye. We hopped into the car and it was the loneliest ride of my life. When we got home to Conway, my parents were home. My mother began crying uncontrollably and held me tight and asked me what happened. I told her I could not talk about it and asked her to please take care of Catie.

I went into the bedroom and the phone rang. Mother came into the room crying and said that Lilly was calling from Florida. How could I tell her over the phone that her sister had just died in my arms? Lilly sounded so happy, as if she was having the time of her life.

"Dad, how are you doing?" she asked. I remained silent. "Dad, are you there? What's wrong?" I started tripping over my words.

"Dad! What is going on?"

"I had a wreck in the car."

"The new car?" she asked.

"Yes, and your sister is gone," I replied.

She screamed violently and I heard the phone drop. There was a beep from an incoming call.

Her friend picked up the phone and I told him to hold on as I had another call coming in. When I switched lines, I heard Jen's voice. Here I am, with both of them on the phone and needing to tell them what happened.

Apparently Jen was having a good time and had been drinking. She was calling to talk to Didi.

"What's up?" she said.

I informed her that there was an accident. I could hear panic in her voice as I said, "Didi…"

Before I could say anything else she began screaming, "My daughter is dead! My daughter is dead! My Didi is gone!"

I could hear her friends in the background. I was crying and in shock over it all.

Jen finally came back to the phone. I started apologizing for the accident. I told her I could not avoid the wreck, and it was my fault. She said it was not my fault if it could not be avoided. She hung up the phone and I switched to the other line. Lilly was still screaming and her friend was calling my name. I told him to tell Lilly that we would arrange for a private plane to pick her up. I hung up the phone and hit the floor and cried and cried and cried.

The next day Jen called and told me she didn't have the money for a flight from Nevada. I informed her that I would pay for the ticket, and that if I were in her shoes I would crawl back to be at my daughter's funeral. I was so angry! I bought a ticket and called her back and informed her that she had six hours to get to Vegas to catch the plane.

The day of her flight was the day of Didi's viewing. I pulled up to the funeral home in a rented red truck. Six friends from NA were there. These are the people that I clung to in recovery at the time. I sat frozen in the truck as one of them came to the window and asked me what was wrong. I told him that I could not go in. I just couldn't do it, and I drove off. I was too ashamed and too hurt. I knew that I would fall apart the minute I saw Didi.

I drove to the airport to pick up Jen. When she got off the plane, she just grabbed me and held on tight. We did not speak two words as I drove her back to the hotel, which was across from the funeral home. I grabbed her bags and walked into the hotel room.

In the hotel room Jen gave me a hug and kiss and she started to cry. She then ripped her clothes off and ripped mine off, asking me to make love to her. I started to make love to her, but then lifted myself off her and fell to the floor. I started crying while telling her how sorry I was. So sorry that I had killed our daughter.

I thought about the way it made me feel and how my outlook on life was changing before my eyes just by getting these words out of my mouth. I also thought of the girls and wished that they could see me in a different light, other than the father that had put them through such pain and misery.

I had stayed away from them a lot as the time for the Feds to put me in prison drew near. I now know that it would have been better on me and them if I had stayed close to them. But, again, I made the wrong choice. If I had to do it all over again I would have done it differently.

The day came for my baby's funeral, and I could not believe all the people there. I knew then how many lives that little girl had touched. There were my friends from the group, the hospital staff, and Didi's school. It was overwhelming!

After the funeral, everyone gathered at my parents' house to visit and eat. As the girls and I sat there, most everyone was telling my parents how sorry they were for their loss. Not one person said it to the girls, or me. My sister understood. You see, my niece Katrina, who Didi was very close to, was handicapped, too, and she also had died at seventeen.

When most of the people had left, I told the girls that I needed to go to a meeting. I had to get as much out of me as I could.

Dad was mad. He said I was leaving them in their time of need. I told him I would be back. I told him I had to do this for myself. He didn't say anything else. I held my girls tight then left.

A few days later I got the call to go to the Federal Building. As I drove to Little Rock, many things were going through my mind. I wondered what the girls would think of their father while I was in prison. I wondered how their friends would treat them knowing that I was locked up. I wondered about Sydney out west. I wondered if she even knew about Didi. I wondered if I'd ever even see her again. I wondered if she'd ever forgive me for not being a good father. I just did not know what the future would bring, much less the outcome of it all. I guess all people who make bad choices think about them when faced with the consequences of their actions.

When I got to the Feds, I was scared. Where would they put me? Would this be the last time I would see the girls for awhile? It was like a movie that was not finished when I started to walk into the building. It was as if a storm was approaching. I could hear the thunder and see the lightning as I pushed the door open and went inside. It was not the news I thought it would be. It was worse than anything that I could imagine! They told me I had to self-report to the prison in Bastrop, Texas!

When they told me that, I lost it. That was the prison outside of Austin, Texas where Didi was born. The Feds did not care about how it would affect me to know that. They didn't care about the way it would hit me. That was how the government always worked. Who was going to fuck with them anyway?

I just walked down the stairs, and went outside into the storm. The blooms from the trees that lined the sidewalk formed a purple maze which guided the way in front of me as I walked. I started on my way to nowhere. The colors of the lights on the cars showed on the rain-soaked streets on my right as the lightning flashed violently against the glass windows of the tall buildings on my left. The thunder rattled the earth around me. Green from the stoplights showed on the rain-covered streets, too. I was wet from the rain as I walked towards all the people running for cover, and I was not phased by the storm's effects on them or on me as I continued to walk.

As a car slammed into the car in front of it, I just kept walking to the bridge that crossed the Arkansas River separating Little Rock and North Little Rock. All I saw were the green and red colors and the lights of the storm all around me. The purple maze was still leading me in a path to the bridge. As I crossed the street, a car slammed on its brakes so it would not hit me. The driver in the car was yelling at me, but I did not even look up at him. I just kept walking.

Drenched, I looked out at all humanity, and at that moment I knew that it would not be long before I would no longer be a part of what I had become accustomed to. I was going to prison for my sins against it all. My sins were towards my girls, not the government that was sending me to jail, but to four little girls that deserved more from their father than I had shown them.

I continued to walk, heading to my lawyer's office. After a mile or so, I got there, my clothes soaking from the rain. I was cold from the rain, but it had no effect on me at all. My mind was somewhere else as I went up the elevator inside the building. When it stopped on the eighth floor I got off and the receptionist told me to sit down. She rushed off to get something to dry me off. I sat down and started to cry. I fell apart right then.

When I looked up, my lawyer was standing there looking at me. He asked, "What the hell do you think you are doing here and why are you soaking wet?"

I said, "I just came from the federal building. They told me I was going to Austin. Do they know, or do you know what that is? That's where Didi was born!"

He just stood there and did not know what to say to me. I asked him to take me back to my car and he did. As he drove he said, "Now A.J., do not do anything stupid, okay?"

I told him I had already done that. All I could see as he drove were the same lights I saw when I was walking; red and green blurs and the flash of lights from the storm. We got to my car and he asked me what I was going to do.

I answered, "I guess I will go to my friend's house and think, or write for awhile. Hell, I don't know. What would you do?"

He couldn't answer because he had never lost a child, much less gone to prison for telling the truth.

I thanked him for the ride and got out, and he drove away. It had stopped raining, and when I got into my car I just sat there for a while and thought of the kids; all four of them. I must have sat there for thirty minutes.

I drove to my friend's house. When I got there I started writing. I didn't say anything to anybody for a long time.

Finally, one of my friends asked me what was wrong.

I stood up and said, "What is wrong? Hell! Have you ever lost a kid in a wreck or been told that you will be going to prison in the town where she was born? What do you think is wrong?"

No one said much to me after that. I guess I scared them. They all were afraid to ask me anything. I told them all that I was just not in the mood to say anything at the moment, but that I was sorry if I said anything to hurt anyone. I don't know if I really meant that or not, but it was clear to me that I was in the middle of hell, and I did not know how to get out.

I knew I was the problem. That's what the people in recovery always told me. If I truly wanted to change how my life was, I had to be willing to change my thoughts of what life was. It was late. I had been sitting in that house writing, and still did nothing to change my thoughts.

I left and drove to my parents' house. I had a home of my own to go to, but I was unwilling to go there for the fear of having to face what my life had become. After driving in a daze, I realized I was going the wrong way. I was near the place that was nothing but pain to me; I was at Didi's grave. I couldn't change my direction, though. It was like the car had a mind of its own, and I was just a passenger. I tried to turn around, but I couldn't do it.

I was terrified that the devil was the one that was really driving the car and it was my time to die. The closer I got, the more scared I was and the more my heart started to race. I started to shake. Was I dreaming, or was this real? I had not been to her grave since the funeral, and I sure didn't want to go now. I was in the middle of an uncontrollable force that was pulling me to the place that scared me the most, and I didn't know why. I thought something or someone had plans that I was not to know. I wondered if it was a joke or a prank. It was not funny to me. Not at all.

It was close to sunrise when I got to the cemetery. I didn't know how or why I got there. It was frightening to me. I broke down in tears and fell to my knees.

I cried, "Didi, please forgive me. I did not mean to kill you, Baby. I hope you can forgive me. I did not mean to kill you baby. I hope you can forgive me baby."

At that point a bright light was forming just in front of me, and I had to put my hand in front of my eyes for it was too bright to make out what it was. I asked God to please help me for I did not know if it was real or if it was the insane thoughts of a man in fear of the future. I thought it was God about to strike me down for my sins. I looked up and I saw Didi!

"God please forgive me!!!" I cried. I lay down on the ground and begged God to spare me of the guilt of killing my daughter.

"Dad, it is me!" I heard her voice. I heard my Didi! I had my head on the ground and one hand in front of my eyes. I could not believe what I was seeing.

She said again, "Dad, do not cry! It is me."

I said, "I'm sorry, Baby. I did not mean to hurt you!"

"It is okay, Dad. It wasn't your fault. I forgive you!" She was standing up and smiling at me. She continued, "Dad, my sisters, all of them, need you now. Get up and go take care of them. I am where I belong, Dad!"

I couldn't stop crying. The sight was so inspiring.

She said, "I love you, my father. Go and take care, and I will see you again one day. Remember, I will always love you, Dad!"

Then she was gone.

It took a while before I could see, and I did not know if it was a dream, or if it was real. I felt better than I had for awhile. My daughter said to me that she was okay and that I needed to take care of myself.

I drove to my home with a feeling that things were going to be okay. That was something that I had not known for a long time.

The day came for me to leave. I had no choice. I told the girls goodbye, and I went to tell my parents goodbye. I told them to take care of the girls, and that things would be okay. I left knowing it was in God's hands now.

I caught a plane and flew to Austin. It was six in the afternoon when I got there. I thought I would just wait around until it was time to go to the prison in Bastrop. It didn't work out that way, though. I caught myself driving downtown to the place where Didi was born. I saw the place where her mother and I had some great moments together. As I walked up and down 6th Street, my mind went back in time. I remembered when Jen and I would just hold hands and think of the future with Didi. I wanted to cry, but I kept my cool and just took it all in. Then I passed a tattoo shop and walked in. I looked at all the pictures of tats and something told me to pick one that would, like my other tats, mean something important.

It took a while to think of what meant the most to me at the moment, and then it came to me. I had gotten my first tat after Jen and I split up. It was a bird falling from a cloudy sky. Then I got one after Didi's death. I had one about my Indian blood. Then there was the one I got when I had taken my life in the ride into space. That was not a thing that I would recommend to anybody if they wanted to live life in a way that they could be proud of.

I asked the guy there to think of a tat that would depict an end to the life that I had lived for the last few years and would represent a turn around for myself and my family. I wanted one that would not only represent a state of mind, but also an end to screwing up. I wanted one that would show standing up for right choices, not the kinds of choices that put me where I was now.

We decided a sun on my right forearm would mean a new day; a day that would give me a chance to change the way I lived tomorrow. So I got the tattoo and proudly went back to the motel thinking that if I did want to live a better life, now was as good as any to start. The tattoo artist told me he had never done this tattoo on anybody. I wondered if God was working a way for me to travel a different path onward through the fog which had become a life of pain, death, and hopelessness.

For years I thought I was superhuman, but in reality I was just misunderstood. Maybe this time would be different, and through me writing about the mistakes I had made, things could become clear. I could turn my life around for the better. I was still that little kid on that ferry in Turkey. It was easy to give in, but this time I felt that through writing, I could open up my thinking to a better way. I could see that I had been standing still, which is the same as going backwards.

When morning came and it was time to go to the prison I somehow felt different. I didn't know why. I took all the words and poems that I had written. I caught a cab and went to prison, uncertain and confused about how it would be. I walked up to the gate and told the guard my name. I told him I was to report with my paperwork.

When they opened the gate which had big steel bars all around and barbed wire through each part of the fence, I knew that I was in uncharted territory. There was no turning back now. My life would never be the same again. This was a situation that would separate the men from the boys. As I walked through the gate, I realized I would soon find out what kind of person I was, and if I had what it took to go forward with a better life. I would either do that, or I would become the crimal that people thought I really was.

"Boys, it is nut cutting time!!!" The guard took me into a holding cell so they could make sure I didn't have any drugs. Then he took me to a cell I would call home for awhile. It took about 45 minutes for them to go through my things. Then, they went through the drill of do's and don'ts in the prison. I somehow found that to be funny.

I found myself thinking about the time when I would get the hell out of here and go home and try never to come back. They completed my body search which was just the highlight of my day. I could have gone the rest of my life without that experience. The guard asked if there was any reason that I would not be safe out in the main population of the prison. I told him only to get out in 18 months. If that is a reason for me not to go in then take me back outside! He did not find that to be funny, and he told me he'd be watching me! I laughed and that just made him angrier. Well, shit! This wasn't my first time to be locked up and the bad boy part he was playing wasn't working on me. After a few more questions he left, and I sat there waiting for them to bring me my clothes I would wear while I was there.

It was time to go out into the yard with all the other guys there. Boy, did I get a lot of looks! I felt like they were thinking I was either fresh meat or maybe the reason they were there. Either way, it wasn't pleasant.

Then the guard took me to my cell. Most of the other guys there didn't speak English at all. That first night was the most difficult one I had. The next morning I got into a fight with some of them. I think their purpose was to see if I was a punk or a man. Well, they got their answer as I quickly got my ass whipped. But, that was the last time that anybody gave me any shit. No one really wins in that situation, but the man who stands his ground gets respect. That's how it is.

The work I did in prison was landscaping. That was great because we were the only ones who could go all around the prison. Everyone else had to stay right where their job was until it was time to go back to the cell. If a prisoner didn't show up where they were supposed to be in five minutes, they were put in the hole. That was not a desirable place to be.

In the hole, you had no clothes, and without warning you'd get hosed down with cold water with a fire hose and then they'd leave you for awhile, and then start all over and do it again. They did that until it was time for you to get out of the hole. And that was up to the man, not you.

I noticed the Native Americans in prison were allowed to go to sweat, a spiritual activity. Knowing I had Cherokee blood in me, I decided to change my religion to Native American so I could go. That would be a way to try to get the thoughts of guilt out of my mind. Those thoughts were still clouding my mind. It had only been a couple of months since Didi's death. I was a little scared at first, because the Indians could tell if you were sincere in wanting to learn their ways.

I went to the place where they gathered. I got a lot of looks. I felt like they were wondering what I thought I was doing there being a white man, but I could take that. It didn't take long before they welcomed me into their group. They were very spiritual, which was exactly what I needed.

One has to earn their way into the sweat lodge by cooking the meals for the others, building the fires, cleaning, and other chores. It took some time, but I earned my way in. It was an honor to be invited into the sweat lodge. It is hard for me to describe the impact it made on my life. I met some great people during that time, and they will always be with me through the journey of my life. The spiritual nature of sweat was as uplifting as anything that I had ever encountered in my life.

While in prison, I also made friends with my cellmate who was from south Texas. It is hard for me to describe him, but try to imagine a white guy as big as a house who spoke better Spanish than English. He was crazy to boot. That was my roommate.

I remember one night, in the middle of the night, asking him about my poems. He asked me why it was so important for me to write about thoughts that took me back through my troubled times which were over and done with. I told him about my girls and who they were and where they were. I told him that writing also gave me a way to make money. I would write poems for wives and other family members of the guys in prison. That allowed me get into all types of groups that not just anybody could. I made some really good friends in the process.

I worked out all the time I was in prison, too. I walked, played basketball, and lifted weights. I fell in love with lifting weights. It was a way to get my frustration out. All in all, prison was not as bad as I thought it was going to be.

I found a way to tie my tattoos together. Sweat helped me with that. It helped me put my life in order so I could explain it through the tattoos. Without sweat, I don't think I would have had the spirit to do it. It helped me find myself. I would make it through. I considered sweat the same as going to a meeting. Things became more grounded for me.

The writing helped me, too. I could say on paper what I couldn't say out loud without crying. My life had turned into a blind man's journey driving through rush hour traffic. My life had become unmanageable with all the things that had gotten me into prison to begin with.

I thought, as long as I am here, I might as well do it right. I didn't want to be a part of the game anymore; the game that only ends with death. I concentrated on getting better. I wanted to get back to who I was, not who I had become through my using.

My buds that were Native American were great. Two of them became my best friends through all their teaching. Their teaching was something that had been missing from my life for a long time. I became trustworthy, too. That's quite a change for a guy whose family would not let him get within 100 yards of them when he was using the most; the time before Didi's death.

The contact that I was building with my Creator became the foundation and the motivation which would carry me through my stay in prison. I can only thank my friends who I sweated with for getting me back to being myself again. There were good days and bad ones, but I made it through.

I remember the first time Mom and Dad brought Catie down to visit me. I wanted to see them so very much. I built the visitation up so much and I could hardly wait to see them. I did get to visit them, but according to prison rules, only for a short time. After they left, it was a long walk back to the cell. It was hard to bear. I was not alone. Other prisoners said they were glad their family could not visit because they didn't think they could face going back to their cell after a visit.

I didn't know how the other prisoners who had visitors often could stand it. The Cubans, on the other hand, never had any visitors. They were crazy mothers. The government never gave them any hope of getting out. They didn't care how they acted. They had nothing to care about. They'd get killed right in front of the other prisoners. But, technically, no one died on the prison yard or in the prison. The guards would wheel the dead outside the fence and then they'd get pronounced dead. What a government we had! Hell! I served for this so called land that I called home. One would think that if I had died in there, they would at least have told the truth about how it happened. But, not in the federal prison; I saw it with my own eyes four times at least.

Once I wrote a poem about the water tower we had. It had a smiley face on it. That face became a thing of hate for some, and for some it became their friend just because for them, that was all they would wake up to for the rest of their lives. I thought about how ironic that was and at the same time, how screwed up it was. Who would want a smile on a water tower looking down on them while they were locked up anyway. It became a motivational thing for us to not let that s.o.b. get the best of us while we went through our time in prison.

Then there was the fence. There were so many softballs, basketballs, soccer balls, and footballs in that fence that one could have made a lot of money selling them. The closest you could get to the fence without getting blown away was about twenty feet. I just had to laugh at how much money our government was spending each week on just supplying the balls for us to play with. It was so screwed up it was not even funny.

I had to let all of that go and get back to doing what I could to get out of there. I had to go back to my life and never come back.

I kept working out all the time. I was getting stronger as each day went by. I continued to go to sweat every weekend and write my poetry.

One of my Latino friends found a guy who was willing to type my poems for me and put them into a book. I was very excited about the thought of putting together a book with what I had written. It became a quest for me of sorts. My friends who read them agreed that I should go for it. I did, but with a bit of remorse because I did not want someone to make money off of what was so important to me. I prayed about it and then I let the kid do it. I was very proud of what I had done.

My mind became consumed with my writings, which was cool. But, I was still in prison, and I knew if I ever was to get anything good out of it, I'd be better off keeping the poems. I might need them if I ever had a time when I was down. I could turn to them for some relief. But, others could read them, too, and get help from the words of my poetry.

Thanksgiving was drawing near. Mom and Dad were planning to bring the girls to visit. I began using more weight in my workouts so I would look even stronger than I was when they last saw me. I felt good because I was better prepared to handle their visit, too.

It was time for me to go to the waiting room where they were. When I saw them I could tell they were happy to see me. We took our picture together, and I remember Lilly grabbing my arm. I'll never forget the look on her face. It was shocking to her that I was all muscle and not just skin and bones like I was before I came to prison. I thought it was funny and rewarding for my daughter to see her dad getting stronger. It was good for them to see that I wasn't dying from the use of drugs, but learning to live without them. As always the visit did not last long, but that was how it was in prison.

It was during this time when I made the most money by writing poems for all the guys' cards for the holidays. I also wrote for others who drew pictures. I would put the finishing touches to the pictures as well.

It was also during the holiday that I got word that my mother fell and broke her hip at the annual Christmas party at the country club. She had surgery, and it went well. But, she wouldn't be able to come visit me, or go anywhere for that matter for awhile.

That holiday season was a worrisome time for me to put it mildly. My mom was the one who took care of the girls. She was and still is the glue that held everything together when it came to the family.

Dad was the money maker. I knew that I had to find a way to get closer to home for them and for me as well.

It was almost impossible to get transferred to another prison, but I had to try. I talked to my Native American friends and they all said to go for it. All that could happen was to get a negative answer. So I did.

I worked hard during the holidays. Every day I either walked or ran and lifted weights. I sweated on Sundays. I worked on poems for a lot of the inmates. All of this helped the time go faster. I worried about my mother, and I knew no one would visit during the holidays.

I wanted to get another tattoo. I wanted one that would make me part of the circle in the prison. It would also go with my other tats. They all would tell a story about my life.

In prison, if you got caught getting a tat, they'd put you in the hole for awhile. That was just the chance I had to take, because I wanted that tat. Also, in prison, there was no regular tattoo gun. We had to make one out of an ink pen with a little motor. It took a little longer than in a shop, and it hurt a little, but it was worth it. The tattoo was on my back. It was the four doors of the sweat ceremony. It put my life story all together. I was and still am very proud of it. It took a while for it to heal, but I did not care. It meant the world to me. It was a good way to be one of the group. It told people about my Native American bloodline.

It became clear to me at that time that I was getting my life back together, and I was doing it in prison. Shit! I was at the point of having my life where I wanted it to be. But, I still had to see if I could continue this healing on the outside as well.

I would have to get the thought of the halfway house out of my mind. I was not that person anymore. It would be different this time. In the lodge I asked for the Grandfather to guide my path. I was getting myself back in the right frame of mind. I wanted to go forward instead of backwards. I worried about what my life would be, but I knew I'd have to cross that bridge later. I still had some time in here before it came to that anyway. Why think about it now?

We all helped each other get through each day. Our friendship kept us from going insane. The guys were my connection to reality. As the days went on we did our jobs and played when we could. We never knew what would come next.

The lodge was the key to my hopes. I will never forget the spiritual value that was given to me; a guy that had lost his way by way of the death of his daughter. I continued to write about all the things that once meant so much to me. It became a cloud that always was over me as a reminder of what was important and what was not.

The chief at the lodge told me that losing Didi was the cloud that was there always, and I would not know the meaning of that until I got out of here. He told me I had to face it alone. His wisdom was always inside of my thoughts. I could not shake them. I was told that wisdom would come in time, but beware of the trickster. In the old way, the trickster was the coyote, the sign that was the heart of one's problem within oneself. I thought it was that I still thought I killed my daughter, but it was the fear of the unkown that was playing on my mind. The thought of what will be. I would not face that until it was the right time.

I had some troubling times. One day a guy dropped dead on the handball court. He was in his fifties and had a heart attack. Another time, one of the Cubans knifed a guy coming out of the gym. It killed him on the spot. I just did my job and worked out and went to sweat. A group of us got into a woodshop for a course in drafting, and that was going good.

Spring came and I got an unexpected visit from my parents and the girls. They were headed to San Antonio. It was almost May and my mom was doing better. The girls couldn't get over the way I looked. By working out, I was all muscle. We had a good visit. My dad asked me if I had heard from the prison officers about getting closer to home, and I told him he might as well count on me being here until December when I would get out.

I didn't think they'd let me go to a halfway house after what had happened the other two times I was in one. Plus, the Feds did not care if Mom had something go wrong. They would have to prove that they could not take care of the girls for me to get out. As far as the Feds saw it, there was no need to move me now when I would be out for good in a few months.

Dad said that maybe I was right, but that he had pulled some strings and we would just see what would happen. Mom was proud of me for doing well in prison and not getting into any trouble. I told her that the last thing I wanted to do was to screw up now. I told her when I got out of here things would be different. I told them goodbye. I thought the next time I would see them would be when I got to Little Rock after I got out.

My friends from the lodge thought it was nice for me to be able to see family. I told them they could come see me anytime once they got out. They were my friends forever as far as I was concerned. It was Sunday and we had a meeting at the lodge as we did every Sunday. We were the only ones that could go early on a Sunday because we were Native Americans, and proud of it.

I did not know that would be the last time I would see my friends in the lodge. When I got up the next morning and went to work things seemed like any other day. I was just doing my job cleaning the grounds. A guard came and told me to report to the office. Usually that means one thing. But, when I got there, they told me I had a couple of hours to get my things and report to the transfer point. Damn! I thought, what now? Where the hell was I going?

I was put on a bus chained to two other guys. We took off to Austin. This was my first look at Conair. It was nothing like the movie; nothing like it at all! I was blackboxed. I had shackles around my feet and hands and waist. My hands were put into a black box. If the plane went down, I would be the only one to be found. I would not be there, but my hands would be in that box. Nothing else would be found I bet.

I had been all over the world in airports before, but not like this. Hell, it was like everyone in the airport could see us being put onto that plane. Prisoners from all over the place boarded. We couldn't say a word either. I think if we did, they'd throw us off in midair. We were treated terrible.

I thought of the movie "Ben Hur". When the ship got rammed, they weren't going to get out alive. I felt like just another piece of meat for the Feds; not human at all. It was not an enjoyable flight at all. We had a couple of stops along the way and then we got to Oklahoma City. That was one of the Fed's big stop-over points. It was not a place you would want to spend your time in. It was a lot like county, but without the jam. Hell, this prison had its own terminal, and it was a fucked-up place to boot.

I didn't know where I was going for a week. Everybody was crazy! At least they thought they were. Some of them thought they were bad, too. The guards set them straight, though. They beat the hell out of them, and we never saw them again. The food tasted like shit, too. I never liked Oklahoma City ever again after that week.

Then, they told me I would be going to Atlanta. The Feds said that was one of the worst places on earth. I didn't want to be there with what I heard was going on at that place. They said that someone got killed in there everyday. I sure didn't want to go there if I could help it. But, it was not my call to make. I wasn't able to tell my parents where I was either. They thought that I was still in Texas.

It took a couple of days before I got out of there and was put back on my favorite airline to go where they wanted to take me. It seemed to take forever just to get on a plane. It was kind of like the military. I didn't know where I would be sent next. It was the hurry up and wait plan of action. As I was put into another holding cell, it hit me that they might take me to a place even further away than Austin. Where would I be sent was the million dollar question.

I only had about six months left, and nothing was going to keep me from getting home unless it was God Himself. After waiting in the holding cell, we took off. Away we went to hell as far as we knew. When we got on the plane we couldn't even scratch our balls much less feel our fingers. If anyone had to use the facilities, well, you just went in your pants. Hell, they did not care. We were the lowest of the low as far as they were concerned; not human at all. So, we just sat there hoping we got to our destination in one piece.

It took about an hour and a half to get to Memphis, Tennessee. We all got off the plane as big FedEx planes, and Delta planes, Northwest planes just drove by. It looked like they were all aiming at us. Then buses came to pick us up. One bus went to Yazoo City, Mississippi. One went to Forrest City, Arkansas, and the third was taking prisoners to Memphis. None of us wanted to go anywhere but home, but it was not to be.

They began calling out our names. I heard my name. They put me on the bus to Memphis. I didn't like it, but it was closer to home. It was a short ride to the prison. I saw some familiar places where I had been as a young child. For a short time, I forgot where I was. I was remembering the past times I had been there.

We got to the prison. It looked like a shitty place, but all prisons were. There were about 10 or 12 of us on the bus. They took us off as quickly as they could, so they could process us before it was time for chow. I was one of the last ones to be taken to the guard to be processed when one of the guards came in and asked for me. He told me to go with him. I followed him, not knowing what was in store. He took me outside. He said he was taking me to the camp. I asked if he was sure he had the right guy. He said I was to go to the camp in Millington. I didn't want to argue. It didn't seem possible, but I sure wasn't going to say a word. How did I get so lucky?

The camp was like church camp. There was no fence. No one was in the woods with guns ready to shoot on sight. I thought maybe I had been put in charge of an outpost like I was back on base in the Air Force. It did not look real at all. I got out of the van and went inside to check in. I asked again if there had been a mistake. The guard checking me in told me that they did not make mistakes there.

I knew then this was not going to be easy at all. There were too many ways that one could get away from this place, and that put me on edge. Plus I didn't like the way the gung-ho assholes around here were acting as if they were the biggest and baddest jar heads that the Feds could find. It felt like a place where a person could get into trouble easy.

When I got checked in, they sent me to the priest who was over the church there. He said he was glad to see me and asked about my religion. I told him that I was Native American, and he smiled and said they had a great Native American group there. He said he'd introduce me to the chief that was over that group. That made me very happy. I knew I could still sweat there. They took me to my sleeping quarters. It was a new thing to be sleeping with a lot of guys like it was basic training all over again. We were in kind of a barracks that about 60 or 70 guys slept in. It was where all the narcs were sent. That gave me an uneasy feeling.

I got settled in and went to chow. They were all looking at me. I knew they were wondering what I had done to be in there.

I stood up and announced, "I was behind the fence for two years and the feds took a wrong turn, and I ended up here. If anybody has a problem with that they could see me after chow!"

I sat down and never had a problem after that. When I got out of the lunch area a lot of guys came up to me and told me that I seemed like a guy that would not take any shit off anyone. They liked that. They introduced themselves and we became friends.

I started working out with those same guys. Most of them were from Arkansas. It was nice in a way to see guys from home. One day, I noticed a sharp pain; the same pain like I had in Bastrop. I worried that something was wrong, but I knew the Feds were not going to take anybody to the doc unless it was life threatening. I just had to put up with it. It hurt a lot. It seemed to be in my shoulder area, but it went down my arm to my hand. I had some numbness with it, too. I loved to work out even though it hurt. Working out helped me pass the time.

One day, some guys were playing basketball and they needed me to fill in. They were much younger. I guess they didn't think a guy in his forties could play as good, if not better than they could. It was like taking candy from a baby. It made them mad because I beat the shit out of them. They wanted me to play them again, and I beat them again. That made it even worse. They did not like it that a guy twice their age could play circles around them, and all the black guys were laughing at them. After that, I couldn't find anyone who wanted me to play with them.

I finally called my parents and told them where I was. They were happy that I was closer, and they asked when they could visit. I told them that it would take a couple of weeks because the list had to be approved. I told them I would call back and tell them when they could come see me. The girls were happy, too. Mom and Dad told me I might have a slim chance to go to the halfway house in Little Rock again. But I didn't count on it because I had been there before, and the halfway house would have to approve it.

The weekend was a thing that I had not had for awhile. Here, we could just go and do anything that the place had to offer. We were able to walk around or play sports. But, as usual, there were always some dumb guy that thought he could outsmart the Feds and try to do something stupid. That guy would get transferred to the prison in Memphis. There he would find out just what it was like to screw up a good thing.

I told the guys if they thought this place was bad, then go ahead and act up and the Feds would find them a place that I was sure they wouldn't want to go. There were still about 30 or 40 guys that just had to prove me wrong. I suppose they had the time of their lives wherever they ended up. As for the rest of us, it was a time of work and play; we did what we could to pass the time.

At the lodge here, they had volcanic rocks. They were best for the fire for sweat. I had to prove to the Native Americans here that I knew what to do. I had to prove myself in order to be allowed in. What caught me by surprise was that the chief here told me the same thing that the chief in Bastrop had said. They both said I was being tricked by the trickster. They both told me there was someone from the past that would come into my life, and I was not to be afraid of them. I was to go with the heart of my spirit animal, and let the hawk fly. That really messed me up for I believed them. I was confused to say the least. What was coming? Would I see it coming?

That was on my mind constantly. I began to think I was over reacting to something from someone who didn't even know me at all. I decided to leave it to God to figure it out for me.

I wrote to a friend of mine and told her that I was in Memphis at this camp. She wrote back that she would come to visit me in a month or so. That made me happy.

I continued to sweat and workout. I couldn't get the pain out of my mind. The thought of going back to the halfway house was scary, too. That's was where I always had trouble being clean. I also knew I'd have to work there, and my dad would want me to work with him again.

I didn't know how I could get back to working with him again. He didn't like what I had become before Didi's death. He didn't understand what I was going through now in my mind. I couldn't get the wreck and how I had failed them all out of my mind. I could never get him to understand what I felt now. I knew I had failed them all, but I had also failed myself.

I asked the Grandfather to give me a sign to guide me. I wanted Him to help me with my thoughts at this time. I wanted Him to show me how to handle it. He had an answer for me sooner than I thought.

Soon after that, the girls and my parents came to visit me. The priest came to the lodge the next Sunday and told us that there was going to be a powwow in Memphis. It would be at a high school football field. I got excited about that. For one thing, it was one way we could get out for a little while, but most important to me was that I would go to a real powwow. Only the guys in our group could go.

As the time got closer to the event, we all got even more excited. We were already going a little crazy around the camp anyway. We went by bus to the football field. It was an inspiring sight to see. All the Native Americans were in full dress. There were also amazing crafts on display. There are no words to describe how I felt.

We watched the dancers all around us. We were in awe of the way they danced. I walked around and noticed a line of people waiting to talk to a lady. I found out she could tell a person if they had Indian blood. She could also tell what a person's spirit animal was. I stood there and waited my turn. I was shocked by what she told me. It was so spiritual. I couldn't believe what I was hearing.

The lady said, "Your family is from Cherokee blood. They came from Johnson City, Tennessee, and you are from Arkansas. You are troubled from your past. Beware of the trickster, for he will play with your inner soul. Have the Grandfather guide you through. The people you care about will doubt you, but do not give in. Even when you push them, do not give in. Do not give in to the trickster, for he is not what he says he is. Do not fear, for you shall find your way after the death of the mother."

I got weak at that moment and had to sit down. Her words were the same words I had heard at the lodge. I couldn't take it. I was afraid.

She continued, "I have seen you before, and the burden you carry is not yours to carry. It was the Grandfather that took your little one to be with Him. It was not your fault what happened. You shall not go into the troubled time without the things you need to live through it, my son. You will find a way out after the death of the mother, so go now and prepare yourself for the journey that you will travel."

I was blown away from the words that the lady said to me. I did not know why she said these things to me. I didn't know what they meant. One thing was for certain, though. I was in for one hell of a ride, and it was not going to be nice. I did gather that from her. But what mother? What did it mean? Was it my mother she was talking about?

I went back to her later. She said, "Let the hawk fly, my son."

I didn't know what the hell she was talking about. But, I knew I better think about it some more before I set off on my journey.

The next week, all I could think about was what the lady had said to me. Even when we were in sweat, I asked if anybody knew what it all meant. The guys said they had never known that to happen to them before.

I had a dream of the lady, and again she was telling me that the hawk will fly. What did she mean? It troubled me a lot, but I didn't let on that it was on my mind at all. So, like always, I walked, did my workout, and went to sweat, while all the time the words that she said to me were on my mind.

    I finally heard from the halfway house. They allowed me to go back there and have a chance to go home if I did the right thing this time. I told the girls and my parents, and they were all happy as hell. They knew it meant I would be coming home after all.

    That week was the week of July fourth. I went through my daily workout like I always did, and then it was time for me to go. It was a tradition that the one who was leaving camp was covered in the coldest water they could find, and he just had to take it. I took all they threw at me and more.

    I was a little scared when it was time to go. I knew that when all my friends from home found out I was home, they'd try as hard as they could to pull me back down. I knew some would try to get the money I owed them. I knew they'd threaten to kill my girls or me. But this time would be different. This time they'd have to get to me through my dad. They knew him and they knew they didn't want him to get involved at all. But, I had to get home first and see what would happen.

    That was my first goal. For me, just to get home was what I wanted to do. The morning came for me to leave. I was ready for sure. I thought of my friends at Bastrop. I hoped they were okay. I hoped I would see them again some day. I thanked the guys at camp and wished them good luck with what ever they had to go through. I got on the bus that would take me to Little Rock where Dad was planning to meet me. I thought about all the guys that I had met along the way from Bastrop to Memphis, and how much they all meant to me. I went through low times thinking of Didi, Catie, Lilly, and Sydney. I wondered then if I would ever see Sydney again. Then I started thinking about the bus trip I was on. All I could think was please do not get killed on this bus! I had to make it home.

    It took a couple of hours to get to Little Rock. For the first time in a long time, I saw some places I remembered from long ago. It made me homesick. When I saw Little Rock, I started to cry a little knowing I had made it through some rough times. I made it through my daughter's death. I made it through the time the judge told me I would go to prison. The will that saw me through this had not failed me. It was the God of my understanding that had seen fit to guide me from being a wreck of skin and bone to someone who found himself.

With the help of sweat, I saw the way to find myself during those times when I didn't know if I could make it.

Then I remembered the chief at Bastrop and the lady in Memphis. What did they mean? What would I face in the future? What "test" would I go through? I didn't have the answers yet, but I knew in time they would come.

I decided to try to enjoy what I had and remember the things that were the most important; the girls. Were they to be with me, or would I be the one that would drive them away again? When I saw Dad it was as if I had never left. He wrapped his arms around me and told me that he was so glad that I was home. He told me he loved me, and I told him I loved him.

He drove me to the halfway house to get checked in, and then he had to go. The rules were that I had to be there for three days before I could go to work. One of the men who worked there before was still there, and he asked me if I had changed? I told him that no one would ever get me to go back to what I was before. I told him I was going to be the best one here. I think he believed me that time, because he said something had changed in me. I told him that I not only had changed, but what I had gone through with my daughter was never going to happen again.

I felt kind of out of place. I guess it was because that I had been locked up for a while, and I was not used to all the noise from the streets around the halfway house. It made me nervous for a while, and since I could not go anywhere for a few days it made me leary of all my surroundings. I found myself wishing I was still behind the fence where I felt safe. I know that sounds crazy, but when you have been there like I was, you can feel the demons all around you when you get out. I just stayed in my room for a couple of days until they let me go to work in Conway.

The drive to Conway was like being in that bus, or on Conair, for I was not in control of the person who was driving the car. I was also worried about being with my dad. He always made me nervous, to say the least. But, when I got to the nursing home, the employees made me feel right at home. They knew what I had gone through to get back home.

Then Dad asked me what kind of car that I wanted to drive. I reminded him that he had told me if I stayed clean and out of trouble, I could get any car that I wanted. So, I told him I wanted a Lexus coupe. He was a little hesitant, but then he said he'd keep his promise to me. In the mean time, I had to drive a company car. That was fine with me.

I had to tell the halfway house what kind of car I'd be driving, and then I had to give them 25% of my gross paycheck to stay there. I had to pass all the drug tests that they would give me. I told them that would not be a problem this time for I had changed for the better. They were going to watch me like a hawk. I told them no one could make me fail anything that would cause me go back to the way of life that had gotten me into this position.

As always, I would have to prove it to them like I had proved it to myself for the last two years already. I had lost not only my freedom, but my child. If that was not enough to keep me from going back, just send me back now, and we all can save ourselves some time and effort. Or, just stick around and I would show them how I had changed. It took a couple of months, but I showed them and myself that I meant what I said.

We all got along just fine until my car came in. I got a weekend pass. My dad had gone to Memphis and got the car for me. Boy it was a pretty thing. It was rally red, and boy it could fly. But the lady that ran the halfway house was not pleased that I got to drive a company car that was better than the one she had. The woman had problems, and she did not like me to begin with. That made for an interesting time for us both. She really wanted me to fail, and I was determined not to give her the satisfaction of that.

As I worked, my thoughts changed for the first time in a while. I guess a lot of people who have been locked up for a period of time get nervous about getting laid, and I was not any different when it came to that. I started to go back to the meetings. They were in Maumelle now. When I got there I felt a change in the people. I wanted to get into my recovery again, but it was not the same. For that matter, I was not the same either.

At this time, I finally went to my doctor to see about the pain I was still having around my shoulder. It was getting even worse. I really didn't think it was anything, but a muscle, but when the doctor asked me to have a CT scan of my neck, it kind of worried me. I asked him why I needed a scan. He said I may have a disk problem in my neck. I was blown away. I never thought it would be something like that. When the test results came back it showed that I had ruptured my C6 and C7disks in my neck. I would have to have surgery to repair it. The doctor told the people at the halfway house, and I had to tell my family.

We made arrangements for a downstairs room at the halfway house because I would not be able to go up any stairs for a while after the surgery. It also meant that I could not work out. That was messing with my mind since I loved working out so much. Working out helped me get out of myself, too. That was a big part of recovery. An addict has thoughts that put him in a certain state and that causes problems sometimes. I was worried about my thoughts about going through life on life's terms.

I remember having the surgery and waking up with my mother there. I could not move my neck at all, which was bothering me a lot. I was a little out of it. I didn't know yet if the operation went well or not. My mind was playing tricks on me, too. I had all kinds of thoughts going through my mind. I was thinking about Didi, but I didn't tell anyone. A part of my past was haunting me to the point of thinking I killed Didi. I had thoughts of the people I shot for the cartel. Other thoughts were bottled up inside me and I did not know what to do or how to get them out of my mind.

In many ways the operation was a success, but putting the drugs in me brought the past to the surface again. I should have talked to someone about it, but I chose not to. I thought I could handle it myself. That turned out to be the wrong thing to do. Inside, I was a mess. I put on a front so people would think I was okay. I kept having thoughts of Didi and the things we had done in the past. I would see her on every street corner everywhere I went. I did not know how to get it out of my mind. The trickster was working his demons already, and I could not stop them at all. Demons were all around me.

I really didn't want to leave the halfway house when it was time. I was not ready for what was going to happen to me. I bought a house that I thought was the perfect house for the girls and me. As the Christmas holidays were here, everything was good, but me. I stopped going to meetings and thought I could make it on my own. My family thought the same thing. As far as they were concerned, I was okay now.

The girls began to notice that things were not okay. I told them I was fine, but I was like a stick of dynamite waiting for the fuse to be lit. Then one day something happened that I had been hoping for. I wasn't ready for it, but it happened. I saw Mary in a restaurant in Conway. When she first came over to me, I thought I was having a dream. But, it was her.

She said, "Hello. How have you been?"

"Good," I said. "I thought you were in Washington State."

She told me that she and Sydney moved back the year before. I told her to call me. I told her I was living in Conway. I couldn't believe she was here in Conway, much less with Sydney.

I began to think about what the lady and the chief had told me in prison and in the powwow. Was that the "Mother" they told me about?

I was getting more confused every day. My thoughts were playing tricks on me. I didn't know what was going to happen, but I had a feeling it wasn't good. That made me almost crazy.

Lilly was a senior in high school, and Catie was the little shit she was and will always be. She was a good girl, but the older she got, the more she held on to me. That bothered me. She was a lot like me. She blamed herself for what happened with Didi. I think they had an argument about who would sit up front that day. I know she wished she had told Didi how much she loved her before she died. That was a burden we both had to bear. As for me, it was still playing games with my mind.

I knew I would never fully get over the death of my daughter, but I knew I had to move on with my life. I reached the point when I knew I had to make peace with it and go on. I hoped it would come, but for now, it was the fuel that made my mind a confused mess when I ran into Mary. I couldn't see the effect it was having on me.

For some reason, I just wanted to die. I did not know why or how it had come to that after what I had gone through to get out of jail. I had done all that writing about my feelings and how I thought I felt better about myself at that time. The group in Bastrop and Memphis had helped me go through all of it. I thought it was over. It just did not make any sense that I would feel so bad about myself at this time when I should have been feeling so good about being free.

But, I wasn't; not me. It was as if the front I was putting on was forming an oncoming storm that was building inside my head. It had to run its course. I prayed about it all the time. My nightmares were back, too. They were about the wreck, or about what I had done while in the Air Force, or about the cartel. I knew they were driving me insane. All I could see everywhere I went was Didi and death, death and Didi. There was no stopping it, or them. There was no end to it in sight!

I would ask my higher power everyday, but there was no answer. That made it even harder on me to clear my mind. Jen called once and I told her of my nightmares. She said I had done things on my own for too long now. She said I needed to go back to a meeting. But, it was not the same. It was not helping me get rid of the continuing nightmare controlling my life.

I dreamed one night about the lady in Memphis. I was in front of her again. She was saying, "Until the death of the Mother."

"What Mother? My Mother? Who? Who?" I yelled to her.

I wanted to know now! Not later!

One day, long after I had seen Mary, she called me and asked if I wanted to see Sydney. Of course I wanted to see my daughter! I was scared to death. The idea of my daughter seeing me at that time was frightening. But, I could not say no.

When Mary brought Sydney over, it was as if I had seen an angel. Her sisters were very happy to see her, too. I was nervous. What would I say to this beautiful little girl of mine, and how would she know me. I was so consumed with not saying the wrong thing, like an ass, I asked Mary if she wanted to see the house.

That hurt Sydney because I should have thrown my arms around her. I should have said things that I wanted to say; and that was that I loved her. But, no. I asked her mother if she wanted to see the house. What a bone-headed move that was! The girls got to know each other, but all I did was say hi.

Mary and I were thinking of getting married, but my parents hated her. They still did not believe that Sydney was mine. I knew that she was.

Then Didi's birthday came. Again, I got lost, not just from the girls, but from myself. I couldn't handle the thoughts anymore. I became spiritually lost to the demons inside of me. Again, I just wanted to die.

The physical part of me was being ruled by all the dealers that wanted their money, and they were intent on getting it no matter what it took. They had already said that they were going to kill everybody if I did not pay them. So, I did what I thought was the right thing to do. I left and didn't come back for a month.

By the time I returned, Sydney's grandfather had taken her. Lilly had taken all the furniture and sold it and gone to Nevada to be with her mother. Then I found out that Lilly was in love with a guy named Ray. I had thrown away all that I loved! I wanted to die.

This became what the lady and the chief had warned me about. I was warned not be swayed by the trickster and do what God wanted, not me. But the demons that were everywhere did not let me go. The demons were the dealers that wanted my money and the ladies of the night I was around all the time. They were sucking the life out of me like leaches. Those were the tricksters that I had been warned about in my dreams.

Mary hated me. Sydney did not care about me; I did not give her reason to. Catie and Lilly had seen this before, but not the way that it was this time. I thought I deserved nothing but to die. Then they all could be done with this shit of a father. I was a guy who had done nothing but give them pain and death in their lives. My kids were ashamed of me. They were ashamed of the way my life had turned out.

It was because of my choices that I had made with them. I blamed myself for everything that was wrong in the world, and I got bitter with life in general which made me just want to die even more. That was my last resort. Hell, I had already shot myself once and that did not work, so why not let someone else do it for me. I thought the dealers would finally put a gun to my head and finish the job that I wanted done anyway.

I didn't realize that I had PTSD!

The drug dealers didn't do what I wanted at the time. Instead, they thought if they tried long and hard enough that my dad would give them the money they wanted. But my dad was the kind of man who wouldn't let that kind of trash get to him that easily. Not knowing I was just their prisoner anyway, he told them to go ahead and shoot me because I was a sorry cock sucker anyway.

I had arguments with my dad. He could not, or would not see that it was a cry for help from me. He saw me as an addict wanting what I wanted when I wanted it. But I needed help, and I didn't see any help in sight. I had people all around me who wanted what I could not give them. That was the real me.

I did not know how to reach my dad and he didn't know how to reach me either. He didn't get it, and I didn't get it either. He could not see what the problem was. All he saw were the goones that were all around me. He didn't know I was in the spiritual void that the program talks about. I was so lost that I did not know myself much less anybody else.

In hindsight, I did not know why I was being saved over and over again. I didn't see I had turned from a thief to a begger, asking God to save me. I looked into the mirror. All I saw were the eyes of a stranger not knowing if I would ever get the keys to this jail cell that I had locked myself into. Being lost in the world all around me was like being in a room filled with people and still feeling alone.

I tried to get some kind of outlook for the present. I went to visit Mary and Sydney. I told Sydney that I did love her, but I was being ruled by my past. I only got to see Catie when Mom and Dad let me. As far as Lilly goes, I don't think she will ever forgive me for what I did to all of them. But, I tried.

Lots of things happened during the next few months. I moved into a townhouse. Catie would come over to visit. Lilly was back from Nevada. A guy took off in my car and came back with it wrecked. He tried to give me crack for my trouble. I was so mad I threw him out and threw the shit in his face. I told him I didn't need that shit and to go away. I told him I was going to call the cops and tell them that my car had been stolen. He finally left.

I still had bad dreams and I wished everyday that I had done things differently. I was trying to do the right thing. I couldn't go to the meetings because they moved their location again, and I didn't know how to get in touch with them.

Jen called me and asked me to fly her in to see the girls over spring break. Before she came, I had a dream about the lady in Memphis. Again, she told me of the hawk and how it would fly again after the death of the mother. I awoke. I had broken out in a cold sweat and I was trembling with the horror of the nightmare. It was still haunting me. I still didn't know who the lady was talking about. I became a part of the dream itself. How could I be a hawk if I couldn't find my way as the hawk did? It was driving me insane. I still needed to know the meaning of the dream. I didn't know if it was a curse or a quest. I didn't know how I would find the meaning of it.

I continued to be troubled by the nightmares of my past. They seemed to be guiding me to hell. I left it up to my higher power to guide me. I was not alone in this dream. There was someone else in there with me. I did not know who. I continued to have the dream, and I wanted to take my own life before it came for me in the middle of the night. But, I couldn't do it. I thought of many ways to do it, but I had the feeling that God was keeping me from going through with it. Or, maybe I was just too scared to try. God was doing for me what I could not do for myself. I couldn't see that at the time, though.

I still held onto the light of the spirit even though I had not been to a meeting in such a long time, and I had not worked my steps like I did before. The only thing that was any help to me was the thought of the fellowship that was in my home at one time.

I was being lead back to the rooms, but I could not see it. I was finding my way back. The clouds were breaking up oh, so slowly. There was still a test I would have to pass before I could truly surrender to the fact that as an addict my life was unmanageable.

Jen came and surprised Catie. It was a thing of beauty unfolding in front of my eyes, and for a brief time I was at peace. Jen talked to me after the girls went to sleep. She said she knew that I still blamed myself for Didi's death, and that I had to let it go if I was to overcome my addiction. She knew me better than anyone, but was troubled by the way I could not shake the dreams that were still haunting me.

"You are the best man I know," she said to me. "Please get yourself together, if not for the girls then for yourself, my dear, for you are the strong one, not me."

As tears flowed down my face I held her oh, so tight. Then she said, "Go to sleep, my husband, go to sleep. Have some peace if only for a few hours. Get some rest."

I looked at her and said, "You have not said that to me in a long time, Jen."

She replied, "You have always been the love of my life. It was the drugs that drove us apart, not our love for each other. So, go to sleep my dear, for I will have no other husband. Now go to sleep."

And for the first time that I could remember, I slept without the nightmares. I woke up with the smell of breakfast cooking in the next room. It was as if we were still a family if only for a day. It felt like home again; a dream come true.

I prayed that morning for all of them. The rest of the time that Jen was there seemed to go okay, but the girls did not know what I was going through. When Lilly said she was going back out to Nevada, I could not say no, but I did not like the idea. Jen said that there wasn't anything that she could do. I guess Lilly had enough of what she thought that her dad was doing. So, Catie and I took them to Little Rock. Catie had a look on her face as if to say she was being left alone and no one cared about what she was going through. She hated the idea that she had to stay at my parents'. She had not ever really known her mother.

Lilly had to take the bus out to Laughlin, and her mother had a plane to catch. I told Lilly to please let me know when she got there. I kissed her goodbye. Catie was crying as Lilly went on her way. Then with tears still in her eyes Catie and I took her mother to the airport. Jen gave Catie a big hug and told her that she loved her.

Then she held me so close and kissed me and said, "You can do it. I know you can. You can stay away from those people."

I told her that I loved her and she boarded the plane as Catie and I walked off. Catie asked me then if her mother really loved her.

I answered her, "Yes, she does, Baby. Why would you ask such a thing?"

I held her hand as we went to the car and drove back to my parents' house.

Catie looked at me and said, "Dad, please don't get back on that shit, please."

I told her that there was no way I would ever do those things again. I gave her a big hug, and waved at her as she went into the house. I drove back to my townhouse.

That night, a dealer and another guy came in with guns. They wanted their money, or they would shoot me. They weren't playing around with me any longer. After they pistol whipped me, they got frustrated and took my car.

I went to sleep. I woke up to the telephone ringing. It was Lilly telling me she just got married. I was mad, and I hung up on her. I really didn't believe her. About an hour later her mother called and told me our daughter had gotten married. She was mad. I told her I was going to kill the s.o.b. when I came out there. I went back to sleep.

The drug dealers came back. They asked me if my dad was going to give them their money.

I said, "Hell no! He is not going to give you any money, so if you are going to shot me then go ahead. I do not give a shit anymore."

They hit me again, and with blood running down my face I told them a punk could do what they were doing. I looked them straight in the face when I said it.

I walked upstairs, wiped the blood off my face and yelled down to them, "If you were real men you would have done it already. You won't give me a knife because you know I'll rip you up like meat. The neighbors know you have been holding me against my will, so go ahead, you punks. Go ahead!"

I didn't hear much from them after that. They just took my car and went away again. I went back to sleep. While I was sleeping I had the dream of the lady again. She was talking about the death of the mother, and I woke up in a cold sweat again. I still didn't know what it meant. I did not understand it at all.

Time went on and I got a call from Lilly. She told me that she was going to have a baby. I was not ready to be a grandfather. That night I had the dream again. This time I was really frightened because I thought the mother must be my baby. It must be Lilly. I was scared out of my mind.

A week or two later, I had the dream again. This time, I had a calm about me that was different than ever before. I knew in my heart the lady was not talking about Lilly. It was someone else.

By this time, it was July, and the dealers were still going off on me. But, I didn't even pay any attention because they said everything I had heard before. Then, out of the blue, my dad called and said he was coming over to pick me up. Well, the dealers were not about to let me go with my dad. My dad told me not to rush as he had some things to do first. He said he'd call before he came by.

I decided to take a nap, and I had the dream again! This time it was a little different. The lady said it was time for the hawk to fly. I still felt calm about it for some reason not known to me at the time. When my dad got there, I got into his car and told him not to ever take me back to that place. I told him to call the cops because those guys had been on my case about their drug money that I had owed them for years. I told him I wasn't going to give them anything but trouble. I asked him to take me to his house and let me stay there. He said I could stay.

Then he told me to hold onto myself. I looked over at him and he said, "Jen has had a wreck. They do not think she is going to live."

I whispered to myself, "The death of the mother!"

My dad asked what I was mumbling.

I said, "Nothing, Pop."

Dad said he was taking my mom and Catie out to see Jen. He told me that Lilly was going crazy trying to get to Tucson where Jen was in the hospital, and he told me he didn't think it would be a good idea for me to go.

"Why?" I asked.

"I think seeing her in that shape will make you go back on drugs, and you have come so far even though you've been crazy with all these guys around you. I just cannot see you going."

"Then I will stay at your house until you all get back," I told him.

I talked to Lilly, and she was in tears. She was getting ready to go to Tucson to see if her mother had any chance of surviving the wreck. Jen's boyfriend had been killed instantly. I asked if they knew what had happened, but she said she did not know much about it. I told her I loved her, and I hung up the phone.

When Mom and Dad and Catie left it did not take long for the dealers to start calling my parents' house. I did not answer the phone. The answer machine told the story. As far as they knew, I was on my way to Tucson anyway. Dad had the police go and get them out of my townhouse. They left, and I never saw them again.

I just sat and watched TV and waited for Catie or dad to call me and tell me Jen's condition. After a couple of days they called and told me that Jen was on life support and the doctors were telling the girls they did not think she would come out of it. In their opinion, it would be the right thing to unplug her from the machine. I knew that would be hard on them, so I talked to them as much as I could. I hoped Jen would be okay. But, I knew it would be best to do what the doctors suggested.

I could not believe how calm I was, knowing that Jen had not only been my best friend but also the love of my life. I seemed to be well as far as all the dreams went because they had stopped, and I felt a spirit that I had not felt before. My self-confidence was back, and I no longer had bad thoughts, and there were no dealers all over me. It was as if I had been saved. I had no desire to die anymore. I realized this feeling was something that I alone must feel. I couldn't make it happen. It had to happen naturally. No one could know what I was feeling.

On the other hand, I was hurting for my girls. I was praying that God would take care of Jen in her time of need. The girls called me later and were both crying. They did not know what to do or how to handle it either. They wanted me there. They were mad that my parents did not let me come. I told them that I was here to let them know that their mom was in God's hands now. I told them they had to be strong for each other.

Then Lilly told me Jen's parents were not treating them nice, and they were mad at them. I told them Dad would help them with that. The doctors would know that whatever was to be done was up to them as Jen's children. I told them to call me if they began to feel alone again. I knew it was so hard on the girls, especially since I wasn't there. I felt helpless. I couldn't do anything to help my kids with their pain at that time. Thank God my parents were there. I do not think that the girls could have made it without them. All I could do was to talk to them on the phone and tell them what I thought Jen would want them to do.

After a couple of days they had to take her left leg off just to get her stable. Then they could watch her and see if she was going to come through it at all. It took a week of waiting before they told the girls again that they thought Jen had no chance and the best thing was to take her off the life surport. So, as hard as it was, Lilly and Catie signed the paperwork to do just that. Lilly knew her mother better than Catie. Catie was too young to remember her mother as well as her sister did. That made it harder on Lilly. But, the fact that Catie was in the car when Didi was killed caused her to feel a lot of pain, too. Catie also felt a lot of pain because she did not know her mother like she had wanted to. Added to all that was the fact that Lilly was pregnant! I couldn't imagine the feelings that they were experiencing. Hell! I was almost 2000 miles away, and I was not there to help my girls. I could only cry for Jen and my little girls in their time of need. It was surprising, but I was able to stay clean through it all. I finally could feel the emotions that all people felt in a time of loss.

The program always said the emotions that we feel are hard to handle when they hit us all at once unless we have a connection with our higher power. That, along with the steps, helps to deal with our emotions. Also, a sponsor can help by guiding us through life's ups and downs as we learn to accept things that life gives us today. All we have is today. This was all becoming clearer everyday. I could better understand all those words now. It was all making sense. I didn't feel alone anymore. I had no more demons surrounding me as I lived each day as if it was my last. I had the knowledge of a God of my understanding, who had my back all along. I was free of the trickster; my strange thoughts and the nightmare were over. I knew that is was time for me to get back into the rooms of NA so I could get better at helping myself and others through the program. The value of one addict helping another is without parallel. My time was now.

The girls called later that day and told me when they took Jen off life support she started to breathe on her own! That was great news! But, I knew in my heart that she would never come back to what she once was. For now, though, it was the news that the girls had hoped for and I was happy for them.

Catie was going to Scotland with my parents. The doctor said he thought that would be good for her. Lilly, on the other hand, was going to go back and forth to check on her mother. The doctors would do all they could for Jen.

While Catie was in Europe, Lilly called me crying. Jen had died peacefully, without pain. I told Lilly I would be out there as soon as I could. Mom and Dad made arrangements to come back early to be in Nevada for Jen's funeral.

Lilly and I made the funeral arrangements together. When we saw Jen's body, I didn't see the woman who had given me hope that day she got on that plane in Little Rock. I just saw a dead body.

Lilly took it hard. She was crying as she held her mother close. She had gotten to be with with her mother before she died, and now she had to bury her as she did with Didi. I held Lilly close to me.

I said, "Lilly, your mother got to see her daughter grow up to be a full-grown woman. That is more than a lot of mothers get. She is with your sister now. Keep her in your heart always. She was proud of you."

We left crying. I thought about all the tragic things I had lived through in my life, and decided this was the most tragic of all; seeing my girls in pain. I thought that should have been me lying there dead. Not their mother. But, that was God's will, not mine.

Catie arrived in Nevada. She was beside herself because she felt guilty about being gone. She had told her mother she would see her when she got back from Europe. She was haunted by the fact that she didn't come back in time. I knew that would be something Catie would have to deal with. I couldn't help her let it go. It would be up to her.

If going through my addictions taught me anything, it taught me that we can only save ourselves. We can't do that for anybody else. It is up to each individual to let go and let God.

I was impressed with the turn out of friends that were at Jen's funeral. I had the opportunity to meet them. For the most part Jen had told them that I was a great father. Jen's brother and sisters, however, made all of us as mad as hell. They came to the funeral high. They even tried to get drugs at the funeral home right in front of us. I just turned away and went inside.

I met one of Jen's previous boyfriends. He was crying about the way Jen died. He seemed sincere, unlike Jen's family. Jen's Aunt Shirley did tell me that she knew how much Jen meant to me, and that she would always be grateful for how I treated her even when she was in her active addiction. I broke down during the funeral.

We drove a long way to bury Jen. It was about 95 miles to the military cemetery in Boulder City, Nevada. As we rode in 130 degree weather, the hearse stopped. The driver said we had to let the hearse cool down. We all got a drink and used the facilities. My father and I could not believe what we saw there. Jen's father started playing the slot machines while we waited on the driver to continue to the cemetery!

I have not said two words to that man since that day. I know I had done a lot of disrespectful things in my disease, but not once did I disrespect a person as much as he did his own daughter that day. I can only hope that God can forgive him of that because I can't.

At the grave, the heat was almost too much for everyone. They laid Jen to rest with full military honors even though she had been thrown out of the Air Force for being pregnant with Didi. The flag was presented to Lilly. As I watched her take the flag, I reflected back through the years Jen and I had together. We had three wonderful children that were so great, each in their own way.

My mother came over to me and with a tear falling from her cheek she said, "It's over, isn't it?"

"What, Mom?" I responded.

"It's over!"

I thought about what she was really saying to me then it came to me, "Yes, Mom. It is over!"

She was talking about my disease and my mind and what I had been going through with all the dreams and all the problems with my thoughts of wanting to die and all the drug dealers trying to kill me for money. She had noticed that even though Jen was gone, I had a peaceful look about me; a calm resolve which was very unusual for me. I had not even realized it! It was at that point that I knew my faith was helping me with the pain that life had put me through. I truly had Him in me at that time, and He is still with me today. Yes, the hawk was flying!

After the cemetery service, I gave Lilly a hug. I knew she was in pain, and I told her I'd find a way to help her better than I had earlier in her life. We went to a gathering Jen's friends had organized in honor of Jen. Everyone donated money for the girls. I thought that was a very nice thing to do for Jen's girls.

CHAPTER 19
A New Beginning

    The next day, we all started home. I knew it would be hard for me to get away from the demons that awaited me in Conway, so on the way home I suggested we go through Colorado and look for a place where I could get a new start. I could find a place to work and go to meetings. Dad thought that would be a good idea. We headed that way and reached Durango by nightfall. The next morning when we woke up we were in the prettiest place I had ever seen. Durango was a small, beautiful town with a college. There were many things to do there. We went up the mountain to find a place where I could live and work and try to get myself back together. That didn't work out too well because the altitude was too much for my Dad with his heart problem. We had to leave.
    We continued east and arrived at another beautiful place. I knew in my heart that this place was where God wanted me to be. It was called Pagosa Springs. It was just down from Wolf Creek Pass. I told my parents right then that this was the place for me.
    We headed on home to Arkansas, and as soon as we got home, I made arrangements to move to Pagosa Springs. It was harder than I

thought to tell Catie what I needed to do. She still blamed herself for Didi's death, and she was still grieving over her mother. I just couldn't figure out how to explain to her why I had to leave. I did the best I could. I told her I had to get better so I could be a good father again. I had to find my way so I could be there for her in the future. I told her I couldn't keep doing what I had been doing. When she said she loved me I knew I would be okay. I needed to see a sign that would tell me that everything was going to be okay, and I thought that was my sign; everything would be okay that is, as long as I kept my end of the bargain.

I made it back to Colorado and settled in. I spent my time going to meetings and making lifelong friends. I worked building fences and housekeeping. Things were going along surprising well.

The weather was getting cool. My thoughts were getting better with each passing day. I believed Didi was looking over me.

I decided to go visit Lilly in Nevada. Things were easy there between Lilly and me. We enjoyed each other. We had a good time together and laughed a lot.

When I was there, I drove to a mall with Lilly and her husband, Ray. We were driving along and I had bad gas.

Lilly joked, "Dad, are you sure you didn't crap yourself?"

Of course, I answered, "Hell, no. It's just bad gas."

When we got to the mall, being the smart ass that I was, I got out of the car and walked with my arms held out like I was some kind of stud. I heard Lilly laughing and I said, "What? Did I shit myself or something?"

Lilly shouted, "Yes! You did!"

I started walking backwards with my arms out again and went straight to the car. We drove to Lilly's in-laws' apartment so I could change clothes. I begged Lilly and Ray not to tell Ray's folks what I had done. But Lilly couldn't pass up an opportunity to embarrass me. I walked in holding up some jeans in front of me.

I heard Lilly as she shouted loudly enough for the entire apartment complex to hear her, "My dad shit himself at the mall parking lot!" Everyone got a big laugh out of it.

She and I had some of the best times we had ever had. We both started to trust each other again. It seemed life was getting better and better. That visit helped our relationship grow.

Back in Colorado, life continued to get better. Words cannot describe how beautiful the landscape was. The colors in the meteor showers I saw were magnificent; yellows and blues; colors that only God could create. It all was too beautiful and too unforgettable for a man who just a few years ago had seen his daughter die in his arms, been in prison, and gone through the death of the only person he had ever loved and had loved him back. I was living a dream that was too good to be true.

I called and talked to Catie and my parents a lot. I could sense that things were getting better with them, too. I had forgotten just how good life could be. I would never want to go through what I went through just to notice how good life could be.

I was getting better and better spiritually. I would at times look at the aspen trees as they turned their fall colors with the snow-covered mountains behind them and think of the people in recovery. I knew I was putting my mind to good use now for the first time. If God would let me, I would thank these people for the gift of recovery, and for their love and faith they had shown me. They had freely given me their help. They thought more of me than themselves. That to me was recovery.

So many things happened during that time that took my mind off the past. I didn't think about my body. I knew I had gained weight. I just didn't stop to think about how much. I wasn't focusing on my health.

Thanksgiving was drawing near. I started my trip to Arkansas to see my parents and Catie. I was looking forward to showing them what my life had become. As I drove my mind began wandering. I looked back at what I had been through. I remembered Didi and Jen and what they meant to me. At that moment, I felt peace with myself. As the mile markers went by, memories came to me as if it had all been a dream; I thought about the things I had put myself and my family through.

For some reason my mind went back to the bad times I hadn't thought about in a long time. I was almost to Texas when I thought back to the time the girls and I were driving from Yuma, Arizona to Arkansas. It was really cold when we got to Amarillo. We had stopped for gas, and I called my dad to ask him to turn the heat up in the townhouse so it would be warm when we got there. He told me there was nothing in the townhouse. I didn't catch what he meant.

When he said it again, I couldn't believe it. I got back in the car and Jen could tell by my face something was wrong. I told her that someone had broken into the townhouse and stolen everything we had. I saw her go from just tired to hurt and angry in a split second.

Now, as I continued driving, I approached that very gas station in Amarillo where I had called Dad that day. The next thing I knew, red lights were flashing in my mirror. Yes, I got a ticket, but I think it was God telling me to let those thoughts go. I didn't need to get caught up in them. My higher power had different plans for me.

When I finally arrived in Arkansas and after seeing Catie and my parents, I had a big smile on my face. I knew I was okay that day and that moment. Catie saw me and yelled out happily. When I got out of the Jeep, they could not believe their eyes. I had gained about 80 pounds. It was a wonderful thing to hear them say how good I looked. I had a great Thanksgiving that year.

After the holiday, I headed back to Pagosa Springs with a confidence that had been missing from my life for years. I arrived with a new sense of recovery and purpose. I continued my meetings. Friends called me when they needed to talk. I even felt needed.

CHAPTER 20
Sweet Life

Lilly was getting closer to her due date. She called and told me she would be having her baby soon and that it was a girl. My first granddaughter would be born soon. I couldn't believe I would be a grandfather! I was pretty cool with it, and the best part was that this new addition to the family would hopefully never ever see me high. I just wished Jen and Didi could be there.

    I stood outside the hospital in Bullhead, Arizona the night of December 22, 2001. I had never had a gift as wonderful as the four girls I had, but now a granddaughter who would never see me as I used to be was about to be born. I remember the minute Alli was born as if it was yesterday.

    Alli was only a week old, and Lilly and I decided we'd all go to my place in Colorado. Ray had never been there and we all needed a break. It was raining when we left, and I was glad I had the Jeep. Lilly asked me if I thought it'd be snowing in Colorado. Ray had never seen snow. I told them if it's 40 degrees in Flagstaff, then it would only be colder as we turned north. The baby was doing fine as we passed through New Mexico. It took a little longer than I thought to get to Gallup because of the rain. It was just getting harder and harder.

We went on towards Durango with a one week old baby that was my own blood, and for some reason I knew everything was going to be okay. It was as if God was driving, and a calm feeling came over me as I drove on through the rain.

We got to Farmington and the temperature on the bank sign flashed 34 degrees. I knew it would soon start to turn to snow. I looked back and asked Lilly how the baby was doing. Alli was asleep and doing great.

Lilly asked, "Dad, how much longer before it starts snowing?"

I answered with a smile, "Look!" I turned the lights on bright and it looked like we were traveling at the speed of light as the snow hit the windshield.

"Cool! Ray! Look!" Lilly screamed with delight.

Ray could not believe his eyes. "Are you sure we are going to make it alright?"

The snow was getting harder and harder and coming down with vengeance. I had to slow down. It was a wonder to behold. All around us, everything was white. Even I had only seen snow like this once. As for Ray, it looked as if he were going to shit himself any minute.

I think he must have asked me if we would make it about ten times. I really didn't know myself. I had to stay calm or we would be in real trouble. I couldn't see ten feet in front of me. And here we were with a newborn in the Jeep.

I continued on at about 20 miles an hour. I knew there was a steep hill right before we got into Durango. I had to be alert. If I missed that, we'd be going off a thousand-foot cliff!

We reached the hill and I slowed to 5 mph. We made it safely down into the town and I turned toward Pagosa Springs. We had 60 more miles to go.

It took a good three hours to finish the trip. Ray got out of the Jeep first. His legs were a little shaky. I got out and helped Lilly and the baby. Lilly was calm and the baby was asleep.

God was my co-pilot that night. We all woke up the next morning to a wondrous sight!

Lilly, Ray, Little Alli, and I spent a memorable week together. I took them back to home and returned to Pagosa Springs.

Winter passed, summer came and went, and fall again was showing its colors. I felt a warmth inside me that I had not felt before. I kept waiting for something or someone to hit me over the head and find out that it was all a lie. Things just could not be this perfect for an addict like me. I could only thank my higher power for that, and I didn't let a day go by that I didn't thank Him. NA helped me get back to the God of my understanding, and I was thankful for that.

The only thing wrong was that Lilly and my granddaughter lived in the wrong place. They deserved to have a better life. Lilly and Ray were having problems, but it was not my place to say anything unless they asked. The last thing I wanted was to get in the middle without being asked. Ray had been in some trouble, and my parents had helped them out. I could not stand to see Lilly go through the same things her mother and I had put her through. We find that life has a way of repeating itself without any help from us. I had to take some action so things would not be the same all over again.

I made them a deal. I told them that if they moved to Arkansas with the baby, I would move with them, and they could have a better chance of raising Alli right. It would be much easier on them. I think I made a difference. At least I gave them a choice. It gave them something to think about. I knew the choice would have to be theirs, but I was hoping for the best, so while they talked it over, I went back to Arkansas to find a house.

While I was in Arkansas looking for a house, my dad mentioned that he didn't like the way I was breathing. I told him it was probably just the altitude in Colorado where I had been living. He sensed it was much more, and he asked me to make an appointment with his heart doctor. I told him after I found a house I would go back to Colorado to move my things back to Arkansas, and then I would go see the doctor.

As I drove to Colorado, I thought about the serenity of the place that I had grown so fond of and would be leaving. But, I would give my life to make sure my children didn't live as I had. For me the choice was not a hard one. It was for my daughter, not for myself. It would mean that my granddaughter would live a better life than her mother had.

I took it all one day at a time and one thing at a time. It was a blessing that I had not only the time but the money to do it all. The people in the program and my parents made all the difference, too. Only with their help, I was able to accomplish everything just in time. I didn't know that, but I was about to find out that it was just in time!

I got everything settled, and as I promised, I made an appointment to check my heart. I got to the doctor thinking it would all be business as usual. I went through the tests thinking everything would be okay. When the doctor came in with the results, he said I failed my heart test, and he wanted to do a procedure to see what was wrong. I think all the color rushed from my face. I just sat there not knowing what to do.

I walked out of there like they had hit me with a baseball bat. I got in the car and sat in shock. My dad asked me what I wanted to do about it. I just told him to drive to Tunica. He had promised a trip to Tunica if I'd go see his doctor. I don't remember saying anything all the way there. I played the slot machines without even knowing what I was doing. I was wondering what the hell just happened.

I could not believe it; another test in life. I needed to be strong, so I prayed thinking of Didi and Jen and what would happen to the girls if something was really wrong. The facts were that I had so many thoughts I could not focus on one particular thought. I needed to get it together or I would not make it through the procedure, much less what the doctor might find during the procedure.

I regrouped and calmed down so that I would be ready no matter what they found. I guess that was God doing for me what I could not do for myself again. After I calmed down, I was able to enjoy the remainder of the trip to Tunica with my dad.

I was extremely nervous the morning of the procedure but confident that it would be something small, or just nothing at all, but the anticipation was still hard to take. They medicated me to the point that I was half aware and half out of it. The doctor did the procedure and came to us with the results.

He said, "Well, Mr. Shaw, you have a small blockage in your heart and another small blockage in your right leg. We can control that with the proper meds. But…has any doctor informed you about your Hepatitas-C?"

"What!!! What did you say?! Hepatitas-C?"

"Yes! You have hepatitas-C! Has anyone told you that?"

I didn't know what the hell! First I thought I had a heart problem, and before I could process that, I thought I was going to die from hepatitis-C. I don't remember much of the rest of that day. I wondered why! I was not ready for something like that, and I was not sure what my Lord Jesus was molding me for.

All I could think of after that was I had to get Lilly and the baby out of Nevada. I had to take care of everything! I had to see another doctor and try to stay alive through it all. Or, I thought, I could just roll over and die. That, however, was not an option for me at all!

So, with God's help, I drove to Las Vegas, got a U-Haul, drove back to Laughlin, got Lilly, Ray, and the baby and their things, and drove them to Arkansas. I had to do all of this in ten days so that I could see the doctor who would put me on the path to getting well. Life was really throwing stuff at me now.

My sponsor and I talked a lot during this time. Without him and my higher power I know I would not have made it through this time in my life. My meetings helped, too. In Conway, I was able to go to even more meetings. Thank God for them! I thought something like this would never happen to me. It happens to other people. But, it did!

It would take another month or so before I could start the treatment for the hep-c, so I had time to get used to being back in Arkansas and to get used to being with my daughter again. Don't get me wrong. As all fathers know, I would die for my girls. But I know also all parents would agree that kids can be a pain in the ass when they grow up. I had three pains! And, I had the pain life can give us all!

After a month or so the medication came in. No one was prepared for what came next. I decided to start the shots on a Monday evening right before a meeting. I thought that would be a good idea. That way I would be around other people who could help me in case I had trouble. The list of side effects was as long as my arm, and I had no experience with anyone who had gone through that kind of treatment and was still alive to tell about it. In fact, I did not know any person who had lived through it.

No one thought it would affect me like it did. In less than two hours it turned me from A.J. into combat warrior. Everyone was the enemy. No one was a friend. It was me against the world and I was going to take someone to hell with me if that was what it took. Lilly got most of the brunt of it. I couldn't stop what it was doing to me at all. I wouldn't even remember it later. I was glad the baby was too small to remember because she wouldn't like me today if she did.

Lilly even said it was like the devil himself took over my body and turned me into a killer that couldn't eat and went for days without sleep.

At the meetings I would rock back and forth with a look on my face as if I meant to kill everyone there. Lilly said it reminded her of long ago. It was the same look I always had before I lost my temper. But this time it didn't go away as before.

I received a month's supply of shots at a time. I took one shot a week. I had three major side effects of the shots; homicidal tendencies, insomnia, and after a few months later adult exzema. The side effects got worse and worse.

One night at a meeting, I thought I was having a heart attack. Someone took me home and another friend followed. They said when I got home I grabbed every knife in the house along with my swords and told them to come on in.

They both said, "Hell no! We will see you later man!" They got the hell out of there.

Another time, I was at a friend's house. They were cooking for everyone. A friend of their son was there. I knew they didn't like the friend. He was bragging about how he knew martial arts. I asked him if he was joking, and he took a swing at me. Well, he wasn't successful. A little later, Catie came in and said that boy had hit her. I flew outside and cornered him against the garage door. It was a good thing that wasn't my shot day. When I took my shot, it was not play time. I still couldn't control my anger. I would've killed him.

One night after I had taken my shot I did something I still am ashamed of today. Lilly had the baby in her arms and told me something about Ray that made me mad I guess. I took a glass and broke it into hundreds of little slivers of glass that flew all over her and the baby. She ran out scared half to death and mad as hell. I fell to the ground crying. I felt so guilty for doing that and I didn't even know why I did it. I called a friend in recovery. She came over with her daughter and helped me clean up all the glass while I cried and hoped Lilly could forgive me.

I was out of control at times and at other times I was emotional and sick. I lost around a hundred pounds or more. I couldn't sleep. I was battling both the medication and the side effects of it. It was becoming overwhelming. It got to the point where either I was going to kill someone or the hep-c was going to kill me.

I remember one night after I'd had one of my calm days, Ray and Lilly had a fight of some kind and Ray went out to his truck. It was a truck my dad and I got him so he could get back and forth to work. He had a tooth pulled and had taken some medication for the pain, and he just passed out in the truck. I forgot he was out there. When he woke up and came in, I heard him at my back door. I thought it was an intruder. I grabbed my K-bar and went toward the sound. I raised the K-bar and got ready. I hesitated for just a second in time to see Ray.

"Don't! It's me!" Ray shouted down on his knees.

"I'm sure glad it's you, or you would have been dead!" I said. I don't think he thought I could move that fast. I don't think he thought I could attack and be ready to kill without remorse either. I know he was careful not to do that again as long as I was around.

I did not know how long I could keep up with the effects of the interferon, but I kept going to meetings and doing what I had to do to keep clean. I had to go to another doctor to find a way to get some relief from the eczema, and on top of the other medicines I was taking he started me on prednisone which made me even more violent. I was in such a state of disarray that the doctor who put me on the medicine for the hep-c decided to take me off it because he did not want to have to go down to the jail and find out that I had killed someone! It was really doing a number on me.

In his words, he said, "You need to get your affairs in order. I don't think you are going to live through all of this."

I took another blood test to check my levels and had to wait ten days for the results. Those ten days were as long as any ten days I had gone through in my life. I was nervous when I went back for the results. I waited in the exam room to find out if I was going to die or not. While waiting, again, I couldn't stop the thoughts of Didi, Jen, the girls, Mom and Dad. I thought about other people who had already lost their lives from this disease. A lot of things were whirling through my mind. The doctor finally came into the room. The look on his face was puzzling. I was scratching all over from the eczema.

Finally he said, "We cannot find it at all!"

"What?" I couldn't process his words.

"Your levels are completely normal!"

I shouted, "You mean it's gone? Test me again!" I stuck my other arm out and insisted.

He said he'd have to test again to make sure there was no mistake. They took more blood, and in ten days the results came back negative again! The doctor and I could not believe it. I did not have it at all anymore.

I have been tested every three to six months since then and I continue to be completely free of it.

One night a few weeks later, I did not feel well at all, and I asked Lilly to take me to the hospital. I knew something was wrong but I didn't know what it was. I feared the hep-C had come back. Right away, the doctor admitted me. I was thinking the worst too, and no one would tell me what the hell was going on. I was just about to explode when a nurse came into my room, started an IV and told me my blood sugar was way out of range. I was now a diabetic. I thought to myself, what else, Lord.

After a couple of days in the hospital, two weeks of giving myself insulin shots, and about three weeks of pills, my levels were back to normal. To this day, I have not had to take anything else. I sometimes wonder how that could happen. I know it was God again doing for me what I could not do for myself. I guess God thought it would take a barrage of bad things to get me to realize I needed Him for the long run, not just until I got out of the next jam. I had to continue in recovery. I just had to! Soon after, I went to an NA function and saw an old friend I hadn't seen in years. I walked up to her.

She looked at me as if she had seen a ghost.

"A.J.?" she said.

"Hi, Claudia," I said back to her.

"You are dead!?" she said in a not quite sure way.

"No. I am alive today." I told her.

She touched me and then gave me a big hug. She told me that someone had told her that I was dead. They told her I died of AIDS!

I laugh and told her, "No. I truly am alive, in fact, more alive than I have ever been!"

THE END

Epilogue
Without the steps, the God of my understanding, and all the people in my life, I would not be alive to tell this story. I live with gratitude and hope because of the promise of freedom from my addiction that was freely given to me.

Going to Colorado was a gift from my higher power showing me that all things are possible if you truly believe. I met some good people there, and I am still friends with a special couple who gave me hope. I still have friends from the meetings there. The NA group in Conway also helped me. One person from that group is my sponsor today. I know that through one's higher power, all things are possible. I don't claim to have all the answers, but what I do know is that I do not live now in shame and I do not feel like I have to please everyone today. If anything was restored by recovery, that is it! Recovery has done that for me. I could never have done it for myself. Hopefully I can carry that message to others who are still suffering. I have gone through addiction, the death of my daughter and the death of her mother, prison, PTSD, diabetes, heart problems, hepatitus C, and some other things I cannot talk about. Through NA, I will never ever have to hide from myself again. I am still here through the grace of my higher power, NA, the steps, and the people who love me unconditionally. I now must give back what was freely given to me.

Even though I live in a world filled with all kinds of war and violence, and I still have my share of ups and downs like everyone in this world has, I know that miracles happen every day to people all over the world. To be able to see my grandchildren, grandbabies who have never seen me high, much less have the relationships with my girls and my parents that I have today, is a miracle in itself. The important thing is that, with help from everyone, I am clean and still going to meetings and reading the Book.

Recovery has also given me the opportunity to go to other countries. In the process of getting help for myself, I hopefully have helped others. It is an honor to see first hand what the program has done all over the world. Hopefully I will be able to go to my third NA World Convention in the future and hear stories that are truly the miracles of this simple program that has given me so much. It has given me the message of hope and the promise of freedom from the disease. We in the program still have our days, but together we can succeed. We each have the steps to help face any problem that may arise, and we have the tools to solve them if we so chose to use them. Today my solution is the steps that carry me through the days with the hope that I can do anything if I make the right choices and ask for guidance from a higher power.

I look back at all who I have known and hope that God is looking over them. So many of them are friends who in some way have helped me. My relationship with them has not been a waste. I will pray for them all. But the greatest thing that has happened is recovery. I wouldn't have any of this if not for recovery.

My higher power still looks after me and I still pray everyday.

Since writing this book, several years have gone by. It is now 2013. Many, many events have transpired; some good, some bad:

CATIE: While clean, I again made a poor choice in mates. Judy wasn't clean, and she was providing Catie with "ice". A letter from the high school informed me of Catie's truancy. When I called the school to find out what was going on, I got thrown into custody court! Of course, I lost. I lost custody of Catie. I felt like God was just laughing at me. Mom and Dad got temporary custody, and Catie ended up pregnant. Because of her active addiction, my parents sent her to boarding school in Mississippi. When that didn't work out, she came back and I regained custody. The courts learned that the problem wasn't me, but my ex and Catie. She didn't want to go back to her high school and finish her senior year pregnant. I knew, though, how important a high school diploma is in life, so I insisted she attend high school and finish pregnant or not. I am thankful for Catie's high school counselor who was of great value and helped Catie get through her senior year. Catie hid her addiction well. The influence of my father over her was apparent. He was enabling her as much as he did me, and it just got worse. She had her baby girl, JoJo, and graduated. However, afterward, Catie continued to make bad choices. She is still in active addiction. She has been charged with numerous crimes. She has been in and out of rehabs and jail, and Lilly is raising her child. I have learned that I can't help others if they do not want to help themselves. I pray for hope. All we are given is hope. I can only hope that her beautiful child doesn't fall in her mothers' footsteps.

LILLY: Lilly and Ray had another beautiful baby girl, Candace. Ray unfortunately started dabbling in drugs and going out on Lilly. During one of his highs he drove his new truck, bought by me so he could get back and forth to work, not once, but three times into the living room of a neighbor's house. He ended up in prison. After serving his sentence, he was sent back to Nevada to serve time there for revoking his probation years before. Lilly divorced him while he was in prison. Her life turned out a little bit like her father's. Her addiction was that her "picker" was broken; like her dad, she kept picking the wrong partner in life. Lilly continued to work hard, though. She had a friend, James, and their friendship turned into romance. She gave me her usual short notice, three days, that they were getting married. They moved into one of my rent houses, and for just a little while, everything was rosy. They had a precious baby, Abby. But, Lilly's rosy life didn't last long, and now she lives alone, works, and takes care of her three babies and Catie's baby.

SYDNEY: Sydney was reluctant to have much contact with me at first after she and her mother, Mary, moved back to Conway. During high school, she came over and told me she needed a home-cooked meal. I knew then something was wrong. She told me she had moved out of her house because her mother was drinking and taking pills. I called Mary, but she just told me to go to hell and hung up on me. Sydney started coming over more and we established a closer relationship. Later, her mother overdosed on drugs, and Sydney carries guilt over that. Through all the pain though, she graduated from high school, attended college and graduated in psychology with honors, married a fine young man, and is working to help others with addiction.

A.J.: I have been through hell and back. While on a trip out of state, Catie was using "ice", and she and her boyfriend wrecked my car. I returned to Arkansas, rented a car, and was rear-ended by a bus. My neck surgery from years before was destroyed. I had painful whiplash, and now have painful degenerative disc disease from the surgery and the wreck. I was living on Cokes and Little Debbies and trying to work and help my children. I developed an anuerysm in my aorta, I had blockage, and I had a heart attack. I have developed neuropathy as a result of my diabetes. I have never known pain like this. I smoke more, worry more, pray, read the Book, and call my sponsor often. I still go to meetings. I am in my 16th year and still very much involved. Throughout it all, I never stopped recovery. Recovery is a miracle in itself. I was able to attend my first European World NA Conference in Spain. Through trial and error, I continued to handle life on life's terms. Another miracle happened. My sponsor asked me to write about my life of recovery to inspire others. I had written free verse poetry in my younger days, but never a novel. It has been a very emotional journey on this road to completing my novel. I tried my best to use the computer, pecking with one finger, one letter at a time. The miracle happened one night while I was in the midst of writing this book. A picture popped up on my computer screen. Under it was a note saying this person wanted to talk to me. I patiently pecked out my phone number and typed that I wasn't a computer person. She could call me if she wanted to talk. After she picked her jaw up off the floor in response to being told about my previous life in prison and recovery, she and I conversed that night. You see, her father was a minister. She had never been involved with the likes of me. As we talked, I put a smile on her face and a chuckle in her voice. I went to bed with a smile. I came to realize as I had been praying for other people, a blessing came to me. On October 3, 2009, she became Mrs. Shaw. She is the love of my life, a wonderful woman who to this day loves me unconditionally.

MOM AND DAD: My parents are becoming harder to deal with on a daily basis because of their age and attitude. Their health is gradually failing. I keep in touch every day to make sure they are okay. If they'd let me, I would take care of them. I have forgiven them, and I hope they have forgiven me. I still love them. The wedge they drove between my sister and me is finally broken. My sister and I have a good relationship now for which I am very grateful. Mom, Dad, and I decided to sell the family business. We thought we had a great deal since we knew the buyer. It wasn't long before we were paying big time for that mistake. We are working hard to recover from the burden of that ordeal.

The disease of addiction is not only a killer of souls. It's a killer of family and friends. It is one of the greatest threats to the world today.

Throughout all the trials and tribulations, there is one constant. The consequences of life will hit everyone, but it's what we do with our choices that make the difference. I have made good choices the last 16 years. It all has to do with recovery.

www.ingramcontent.com/pod-product-compliance
Lightning Source LLC
LaVergne TN
LVHW051831080426
835512LV00018B/2811